D1595478

Adventures of a
Highland Soldier

THE GORDON HIGHLANDERS IN 1867

Adventures of a Highland Soldier

With the Gordon Highlanders During the
Second Afghan War & First Boer War
1867-84

Charles R. Martin

LEONAUR

Adventures of a Highland Soldier
With the Gordon Highlanders During the
Second Afghan War & First Boer War 1867-84
by Charles R. Martin

First published under the title
Adventures of a Highland Soldier on Active Service at Home and Abroad

Leonaur is an imprint of Oakpast Ltd

Copyright in this form © 2011 Oakpast Ltd

ISBN: 978-0-85706-659-6 (hardcover)
ISBN: 978-0-85706-660-2 (softcover)

http://www.leonaur.com

Publisher's Notes

The opinions of the authors represent a view of events in which he
was a participant related from his own perspective,
as such the text is relevant as an historical document.

The views expressed in this book are not necessarily
those of the publisher.

Contents

I Enlist in the Gordon's

I enlisted for H. M. 92nd Gordon Highlanders in 1867. At that time I was a bound apprentice and could not with safety enlist in my native town (Inverness), so I made up my mind to try and persuade a few of my chums in the "Clach" to run away from home as far as Glasgow and there enlist for the "gallant Gordons." Previous to all this, about as many as forty young lads like myself used to gather in the evenings in Sandy McLean's, the turner's shop, and there listen to him reading James Grant's novels, which at that time were all the rage in the Highland capital. Sandy was a fine reader, and after reading a certain portion he would stop and explain the meaning of what he had read and make us almost feel we were in Spain fighting with our grandfathers. I will confine my story to his reading of the *Romance of War,* or the Highlanders in Spain. I shall never forget when he came to near the end of the book where it says:

> When the Gordons came in sight of Scotland after their long march from Dover, the cheering was terrible.

Here Sandy had to stop, for he and all of us were in tears. He then said, "I cannot read more tonight," and we all made for our homes. The book referred to is almost all about the gallant conduct of the 92nd during the whole of the Peninsular war.

I had always a love for the army, and after hearing about the 92nd, I made up my mind that I would enlist in no other regiment. I was so determined to do so that I had 92nd tattooed on my right arm so as I could show it to the recruiting sergeant. Some weeks after I had my mates ready to start for Fort Augustus. It was in the month of May. We all (twelve of us) mustered at the end of Tomnahurich street at 4 a.m., and started on our tramp. We arrived at Fort Augustus about 7 p.m. same day. In a day or so we were in Oban, and there took the boat to Glasgow. *The Clansman*. I think, was the name by which this boat was called.

We arrived in the big *toon o' Glasgow* at about 4 a.m. with three and sixpence all told. As soon as daylight came we were at the famous Cross of Glasgow, and in the Tontine with Sergeant McIntyre treating us all round. He was a proud man that day securing so many pure Highlanders, and all for his own regiment. He had a grand time parading us before the other recruiting sergeants. We all knew McIntyre well, for he had enlisted many fine young fellows in Inverness, and was very popular until Provost Lyon Mackenzie and Sergeant McIntyre disagreed. After getting a good meal, we were all marched to Shamrock Street Barracks, and there treated to nice shower bath, and were told to be ready on the morrow to pass the doctor.

Chapter 2

The Pipes of the 92nd

At 9 p.m. we were all ready to pass the doctor. Of those for the 92nd I was the first called in. As soon as I entered, the door was immediately locked, and I was placed in front of the doctor who addressed me thus:

"What is your name?"

"Charles Ross Martin."

"Where were you born?"

"In Tain, Ross-shire, on the estate of Balnagown; but I left there when nine months old and have been ever since, till now, in the town of Inverness."

"What church do you belong to?"

"To the Established Church of Scotland."

"Are you married?"

"No."

I afterwards was very strictly inspected and passed with flying-colours, as Sergeant McIntyre has it. The rest of my chums passed in the same manner, and before dinner that day we were all sworn in. We remained four days in Glasgow, and afterwards proceeded to Dublin to join the regiment. On our journey there Sergeant McIntyre promised that we would all get into the same company, but in this we were disappointed, for we were scattered all over the regiment. The day after our arrival we were all taken before the colonel, who addressed us thus:

"I am informed by the Sergeant-Major that you are all fairly educated. This being the case, you are sure to do well, if you pay attention to your duties. I am glad to see such a fine lot of young fellows join. You have every appearance of becoming good soldiers, and I am sure you will make your mark in the regiment. Sergeant-Major, see that these lads are put beside good old soldiers."

McGillivray and I were posted to Captain McKay's company, a most handsome Highlander, and one who would not allow one of his men to go to church on the Sabbath without his Bible. The second day after I joined (I will now confine my story to what becomes of myself as we are now separated,) I was ordered to turn out for drill. The day after we arrived there were about ten different squads on the square, and it was only now and then I could get a chance to catch a glimpse of McRae or Cameron. If I looked to the right or the left the drill-sergeant would shout, "Look to your front, that man!" "Johnny Cope" is the dress for parade for the 92nd, and at the first sound of the pipes I was out after them, and followed them all over the square. (I believe the pipes is the first music ever I heard.) And again at sunset I was out with them, rain or shine.

One evening in Curragh Camp, Ireland, they were playing off retreat and it was raining very hard, and after the pipers were dismissed the pipe-major came up to me and said:—

"You must be a fool to come out in a night like this to hear the pipes."

"Oh, I don't care for the rain as I like to hear them."

"Would you like to be a piper?"

"Yes, but how can I?"

"I will see your colour-sergeant tomorrow, and he will put you beside Piper Macgregor, who will teach you, and if you make any signs of becoming a good piper I will take you out of the ranks."

Two days afterwards I was taken away from big Jock Fraser, who was appointed to teach me how to soldier, and put beside a real Clach boy, Piper Gregor Macgregor, (now pipe-major of the Caledonian Asylum, London, [as at time of first publication].) Gregor was very kind to me, and took great patience with me in learning the pipes: but I was still at recruit's drill, and it was only after retreat that I could get my lessons. In three) months I was able to play a strathspey reel and four or five quicksteps. This was just after Christmas, and all the companies were preparing to have a grand dinner on New Year's day. In my next I will tell you the best way I can how the sons of dear auld Scotia spend the New Year in the British army.

CHAPTER 3

Hogmanay!

There are none of the Highland regiments pay any attention to Christmas day, and if quartered along with an English or Irish corps the Highlanders take up the duties of their English and Irish comrades on Christmas day, and they in return take up the duties of the Highlanders on New Year's day, so as to allow all to join in the festivities of the day.

In the "gallant Gordons" New Year's day is the greatest day of the year. St. Andrew's day is not known among the rank and file. Waterloo day has long died out, except in the officers' mess. Every company in the regiment has a grand dinner on New Year's day, and is given as much as one ration of beer per man, and as much as four or five glasses of the best mountain dew. Consider all this with the best dishes that can be produced and you can realize what sort of table that is put before "the lads wi' the kilts."

On Hogmanay night to go to bed is out of the question. Any man seen sleeping is at once called to his feet, for all are anxious to see the old year departing and the new one coming in. About 11 p.m. all the pipers are called, in full dress, to the officers' mess. After the last stroke of twelve the band plays, "Here's to the year that's awa," and afterwards "A gude new year to ane and a'." Then the procession is formed, headed by the band, and march right for the officers' mess, before we make our appearance the tables are cleared and we find our gallant commanders dancing to the sound of the pipes in the most perfect manner. As we enter the vicinity the officers all come rushing out and receive us with a hearty cheer. Then we all mingle together, talk about the other's kith and kin, and if he is a Macdonald or a McKay, or a Cameron, he, the private of the same name, holds that he has the same blood flowing in his veins. This is the general talk among the officers and men. The best of goodwill prevails, and presently Jock McKay or someone else will shout to Major McKay for a Jacobite song. The song is sung and five or six hundred voices join in the chorus. The sight of all this is, to say the least, superb. Just fancy six hundred sons of auld Scotland, armed with sixteen splendid pipers who can play like one man, and a band of sixty first-class musicians playing the very best of scotch airs, and you have an idea of how our brave kilted warriors celebrate New Year's day.

On the first of January, 1868, while stationed in the Curragh Camp, Ireland, we were in the middle of all this when an orderly came galloping into our lines and ordered the bugler to sound the assembly. At the last sound of the bugle some thought it was a false alarm, but presently the orderly sergeants came rushing in saying: "Pack up every man with field kits only, for we are under orders for Cork and Limerick, the Fenians have revolted." In twenty minutes we were all under arms and ready to march to the station. We arrived in Cork about six a.m. on Sunday morning, and as we marched through the streets with the band playing, "Scotland the Brave," you could plainly hear them say, "What a foine body o' men," etc. The appearance of the Gordons in Cork put a stop to all the disturbance, and, as the Chief Magistrate said, the moral effect of the Highlanders did a lot of good to the city.

Two weeks' stay in Cork and we are off to India. And to see us parting with our Irish sweethearts the day we embark will go to show how well liked the 92nd were in the famous city of Cork. Next week will find me far away at sea, and tell you how a soldier fares when so placed. You will be surprised to see how many can go aloft when any sign of danger appears.

CHAPTER 4

To India

On the 26th January, 1868, the 92nd Highlanders embarked on H. M. S. *Crocodile* for India. Nothing worthy of note took place during the embarkation, only that big John Cameron dropped his rifle into the sea, and would have jumped in after it only he was prevented from doing so by the blue jackets on the gangway.

After we were all told off in messes, we were afterwards told off in watches. The duties of a soldier's watch aboard ship is to assist the blue jackets in setting sail or stowing sail, and keep watch all over the ship. There are altogether twenty-one sentries on an Indian trooper, and the most important sentry is the one in charge of the life buoy on the poop. The duty of this sentry is that if any man fall overboard he is to throw the buoy over the side. The blue jackets man the boats, and they must be in the water three minutes after the alarm is given. If not there in that time their grog is stopped and extra drill. Twice and sometimes three times a day a false alarm is given for this practice; and it is one of the finest sights aboard a trooper to see those British tars rally when the alarm from the bridge is given. When a regiment embarks on a troopship for India each man is served out with what they call a sea kit. The kit is made up thus: one sea kit bag, one large handkerchief, one knife, two pounds salt water soap, two cholera belts, two towels, two pounds of tobacco, one housewife, etc.

Fire alarms are frequently given during the voyage of a trooper, and it is in these we see the power of true British discipline. Here are a few samples of them. Any man seeing any danger of fire walks (not runs) to the officer on duty on the bridge and tells him where the fire is; he is to tell no one else. In case of a fire alarm, all hands must stand still; no man must move from where he is; no matter what he is doing, he must continue at it until called to reinforce and help at the pumps.

This, indeed, is a very pretty sight. The sailors get the hose, etc., in order, while the soldiers wait until they are called from where they are and posted; thus inside of a very few minutes every man is in his place, ready to throw hundreds of gallons of water on the fire if it might show face. Smoking is not allowed below, and only at certain hours during the day on deck, and each smoker must have a pipe cover. Any man found smoking below or during prohibited hours is punished in various ways, such as seven days' porter stopped, and standing at attention on the quarter deck, while all the rest of his chums are enjoying the weed. Each troopship has an excellent library for the free use of the soldiers and sailors.

Our voyage was very pleasant until we got to somewhere on the skirts of the famous Bay of Biscay. For fully ten hours the storm lasted, and during the stowing of sails and other work about the ship, which was rolling and pitching terribly, many of the Highlanders went aloft and aided the sailors, so much so that we had special thanks rendered to us by the captain of the ship after the storm. It was at night when we passed "Gib," and our countersign was quickly understood. In Malta we coaled, and arrived in Alexandria a few days afterwards.

Here we took train to the Suez across the desert and there embarked aboard H. M. S. *Malabar*, and proceeded up the Red Sea on our way to Bombay, For three or four days' sail land is in sight on either side. It is in this sea that the famous flying fish are seen. Not being able to fly against the wind when they leap out of the water they are often thrown on the ship's deck by the strong breeze. In shape and size they greatly resemble a herring. I never knew any person to eat them.

On the 20th February Private Adams died, just when we had got into the Indian Ocean. Consigning his body to the deep was a sad sight. He was rolled in his blanket with a round shot at his feet. Private Adams was a native of Glasgow.

On the 20th February, 1868, we arrived in Bombay, and from here we were transhipped to three transport ships and tugged up to Karrachee. We had a very rough passage, and instead of making the trip in forty-eight hours we took seven days.

On our arrival at Karrachee we were soon landed and put into a standing camp. The following day we took a train to Koortee, and proceeded in flat boats up the Indus to a place called Sher Shah, some 600 miles. From Sher Shah we marched to Jullendur. It was sometime in April when we arrived, and we all felt happy to see ourselves once more in barracks, for we had had a hard time to get there. Now the scene of my life is changed and I will begin to tell you what it is like to be a soldier in India, for I spent the best days of my life there. It my readers will follow me they will not disappointed in my brief and truthful statement, which will take one more chapter. After that you will find in the field of battle.

CHAPTER 5

Service & Promotion

Just a week in barracks getting ready for the hot season, and we were nicely settled in splendid quarters. The hot season in India commences the 15th April, and ends on the 15th October; during that period no man is allowed out of barracks from 8 a.m. to 5 p.m. The *pankhs* or fans start mid-morning, and continue till 5 a.m. the next day. One fan is in between two beds about 14 inches above head when lying in bed. In the month of June just before the rainy season the heat in some parts of India is terrible, especially in the Punjab. For a civilian to enter a barrack room in India about 11 a.m., would be a most curious sight—you can see from one end of the barracks to the other; during the day all doors are closed, and open at night. Every man is doing something, very few are asleep. Some are writing, some are reading and mending socks, and everything a person could think about, and, perhaps, away in a far corner of the room some fine singer starts a song about bonnie Scotland.

During the progress of the song everything is quiet. At 1 p.m. dinner is brought; by 2 p.m. dinner is over and many try to sleep, but the bugs and the heat prevent you from doing so. At 4 p.m. the *nappie* or barber comes round and if you happen to be asleep he shaves you just the same. These *nappies* are so clever and light-handed that it is quite common to see them shave a man In his sleep. These *nappies* are paid by the men themselves, they give thirty-one shaves a month for twelve cents. Shoeblacks polish two pair of shoes a day for the same amount. The *dhobie* or washerman gives you two washings a week for twenty cents a month, no matter how many pieces you have. A *coolie* will run a message for you for one cent, even though it be two miles, and run all the way.

The drill season in India commences on 15th October. About this time I was declared a trained soldier. I had now full liberty to stay in the ranks or join the pipers. One night at tattoo, Macgregor told the pipe-major that I really wanted to join the pipes. I told the colour-sergeant my intentions, who at that time seemed angry with me for thinking of such a thing. Next day after parade I was taken in front of Captain McKay. "I am informed that you are thinking of joining the pipes, are you very anxious to join?"

"Not very," I replied.

"I intend to promote you if you stay in the ranks."

A few days after I was in orders for lance-corporal. I soon became a good shot and gave much attention to the drill-book, attended the regimental school regularly until I obtained both a second and third class certificate of education, thus qualifying myself for any rank in the army. At five years service I was full corporal, at six I was lance sergeant, and at eight years service I was full sergeant. In 1872, the 92nd took part in the Camp of Exercise at Delhi. Previous to the breaking up of the camp, where over thirty thousand troops took part, there were games held, and in those the gay Gordons carried off more than two-thirds of the prizes. Jock Macgregor, from Braemar, carried away the prize for the light and heavy stone: young Geddes, from Banff, took the hammer and caber; Matthew Thompson, from Glasgow, carried everything with sword and bayonet, including the viceroy's silver watch.

Sergeant-Major Mays, of the 11th Hussars, who was considered the best swordsman in the army, had a poor chance against big Matthew; Colin MacRae, from Clachnacuddin, threw the cricket ball 115 yards; Johnnie Marr, of the 72nd Highlanders, coming next with 105 yards. In the running, McAully, from Paisley, took the two mile; Coulston, from Auld Reekie, took the one mile, and McRae and Davidson, from Aberdeen, took the quarter mile.

Our next station was Chakrata, 10,000 feet above the level of the sea, away up on the Himalayas. While stationed there I took to playing cricket, and, one day, while playing at a match I received a letter from home, announcing the death of my father. This sad news was so great on me that I burst out crying on the field. A crowd soon gathered around me to ascertain the cause of my weeping so much. As soon as it was known, as a mark of esteem and respect the match was stopped for the day. My father was a native of Kennetnmont, Aberdeenshire, and a miller to trade.

After two years stay in Chakrata we went to Mooltan. It may seem strange to say that it costs the Government of India more by troops marching from one place to another, than it does sending them by rail, and yet it is very seldom that troops go by train, except, of course, in cases of emergency. We marched from Chakrata to Mooltan, a distance of 591 miles. "Reveille" would sound at 4.30 a.m., a half an hour is allowed to strike tents, load the camels or elephants (sometimes a regiment has both these beasts of burden), be dressed and ready to march. As soon as the column starts, advance guards, flank and rear guards are sent out. A halt is made every hour for three minutes. Halfway we come to the coffee shops, where we get a nice warm cup of coffee. Fifteen minutes are allowed here.

We reached the new camping ground by 9.20 a.m. The pioneers are there long before the column and have everything ready, so that each company knows the spot where their tents are to rest. Inside of ten minutes every tent is up and dressed to perfection. Breakfast is immediately served out, for the cooks go with the quartermaster the day before. Immediately after the fall in for breakfast the grog bugle sounds; each man has then to drink his dram in front of the orderly sergeant; he is not allowed to carry it to his tent. After drinking he is made to show the canteen by placing it bottom-upward. During the line of march there is no drill except for defaulters and marked men.

No man must go one mile from camp. There are no saloons in India except in seaport towns, and in these no soldier is allowed to enter. Any merchant selling liquor to a soldier is fined for the first time $250. Soldiers in India have more pay than when serving anywhere else, and 25 cents in India will go as far as four times that amount would go in England. One pint of beer for dinner and one after tea, together with a dram of rum is all a soldier is allowed in India. But a sergeant or an officer can drink as much as he likes.

Two years in Mooltan and we are off to Delhi again, this time to take part in proclaiming our beloved Queen Empress of India. This was done on the 1st of January, 1877, in the presence of all the native princes of India and Cashmere. This was a sight I shall never forget, especially the great march past, which started at 11 a.m. and lasted till 4.30 p.m. Altogether there were about 50,000 troops and each British regiment had to pass the saluting point in column of double companies. The 92nd Highlanders had 72 files in each company, and went past like a wall. According to the *Pioneer*, the leading paper in India:

> . . . nothing could match the marching of the 6th Warwickshire Regiment and the famous Gordon Highlanders, but if we are to judge by the amount of applause given to each corps as they came up, then the gallant Gordons carried the palm.

After all the troops passed then came the long massive black column of elephants, in some cases 50 abreast. Altogether 10,000 of these monsters marched past, each native prince leading his own. Two elephants belonged to the *Gakewar* of Baroda. One was said to be 400 years old and the other 370 years old. A large silver medal was given to each regiment present to commemorate the event, and this medal was to be given to the best soldier in the regiment and to be kept in the family and handed down from sire to son. Colour-Sergeant James Drummond, who was indeed the finest soldier I have ever seen, received this medal, but poor Jamie Drummond did not wear it long, for he was killed in battle a year or so after.

After the proclamation the right wing of the regiment went to Seetapore and the left went to Benares. We were not long here until the war in Afghanistan broke out, *viz.*: November, 1878. It was here we first received the Martini-Henry rifle, and soon learned how to use it.

At this time the 92nd was in splendid condition. The average service of the regiments was about 12 years. We had over 400 marksmen, and this same year I was the best shot in my company. Now my very brief account of a soldier's life in India is concluded. We will now away to the wars and see what the raw kilted warriors can do when they are called to defend our noble queen and country.

CHAPTER 6

The Second Afghan War

After the taking of Ali Musjad in the Khyber Pass, and the brilliant victory of General Roberts in the Khuroom Valley, the Afghan War was considered at an end. Although the treaty of Gundamak had been signed, still troops were pouring towards the frontier, and on the 19th December, 1878, Captain Macgregor received a private telegram from Simla, from a friend of his on the commander-in-chief's staff, that the "Gordons" were in orders to proceed to the front and would likely join General Roberts in the Khuroom Valley. The news soon spread all over the regiment, and that night there was great rejoicing, so much so that the natives thought that the "*Gagara Pultan*"! (Petticoat Regiment) had gone mad. On the 20th December the news for active service in the field was confirmed, for that night we were in division orders. At this time the 92nd were in splendid condition, the average service of each man being about 11 years, and numbered 800 bayonets, with about 460 marksmen. Altogether the efficiency of the corps was superb, and, as Brigadier Wilkinson told us when we left his command, we were fit to go anywhere and do anything.

On the morning of the 21st December, 1878, we left Benares in two special trains for Jhleum; from Jhleum we marched by forced marches to Khoat. Khoat is on the frontier of Beloochistan. Here we were soon joined by other regiments. We remained here till April, and during that time we were kept busy learning the arts of war. such as adjusting the sights of our Martinis to hit an object at 1,500 and 1,600 yards, and how to apply a bandage and to carry wounded, etc.

About the 3rd April, 1878, General Roberts came down from the front and reviewed the 92nd Highlanders in drill order, *viz*.:—White jackets and kilts. After inspecting the ranks, he ordered the colonel to do some movements, this we did to perfection and ended up our inspection by advancing in line, which was admirably done. We were immediately formed into square. General Roberts gave us great praise, not only for our smartness on parade and our grand martial bearing, but what struck him most was the stalwart appearance of the regiment. He said:

> In a few days you will be in the enemy's country. Your gallant countrymen, the 72nd Highlanders, more than distinguished themselves in the late engagement, and I feel sure you will also add much glory to the British arms. I never saw a finer body of men under arms, and I feel proud to have such a famous regiment under my command.

After shaking hands with the colonel and the rest of the officers. General Roberts returned to the front that night under a strong escort of the Bengal Cavalry.

About the 17th April, orders were received from headquarters that the 92nd Highlanders proceed with all haste to join General Roberts at Ali Khyle, (the house of God). After some hard marching we arrived at this place about the 25th April, and received a grand reception from our countrymen, the gallant Seventy-Twa. We remained in Ali Khyle till the latter end of September, out during that time we were continually surveying the country for miles round, and our camp was strongly entrenched. Although no fighting of any kind took place here, still we were much bothered at night by the hillmen firing into our camp. At night we had a cordon of sentries round our camp with outlying picquets and inlying picquets. All sentries were loaded, and were doubled at night.

The orders of each sentry were: to keep a sharp look out in front: challenge all persons twice; should the second challenge be disregarded, to fire. While sentry No. 1 was challenging, sentry No. 2 was covering the object. This is a sample of how a sentry challenges in front of an enemy: "Halt! Who comes there?" "Halt, or I'll fire!" If it be rounds, he would say, "Visiting rounds." Sentry would then say, "Stand! visiting rounds, advance one and give the countersign." Rounds would then advance slowly and whisper "Edinburgh," or whatever it was. On outpost duty, rain or snow, every sentry is sharp on the alert, and night sentries never fix bayonets, or move about. The double sentries are ten yards apart, so that a chain goes right round the whole camp. This being the case every man that is not on duty knows when he lays down at night he is well guarded and he can sleep sound.

Sometime in July Major Cavagnari and his staff passed Ali Khyle on his way to Cabul. It was agreed in the treaty of Gundamak that Major Cavagnari, with three other officers and 75 troopers of the guides, as an escort, should remain in Cabul and be under the protection of the *ameer*, Yakhob Khan, the new king. After a few weeks' stay in Cabul, the whole city, together with six Afghan regiments, headed by the new king, attacked Major Cavagnari and all his train and murdered everyone of them. Three days after this cruel affair the news reached our camp; then the cry for vengeance came from all quarters, and in less than twenty-four hours after the sad news reached us, we were marching in hot haste to Cabul.

On the 5th October, 1879, we sighted the enemy for the first time, and after the cavalry scouts came back that night they reported them as being strongly entrenched on the hills and valleys near the village of Charasia, with about twenty guns. That night I was on the main guard and we could plainly see the camp fires, etc., of the enemy. I thought to myself of the glory that was now before us, for we were all burning for vengeance, and the "Gordons" were exceedingly happy to learn, on the morning of the 6th October, that they were to lead the advance. All the crack shots were picked for the long ranges, and I was one of them.

It was on this day, the 6th October, 1879, that I fired the first shot against the enemies of my country, but whether I struck object I aimed at I cannot tell, now the war begins, and our battle is going to commence, in my next I will tell you result.

CHAPTER 7

The Hills of Charasia

By five a.m. the whole of General Roberts' little army was on the move; by five-thirty a.m. we were within range of the enemy, and although the Afghans were pelting at us as hard as they could, we seldom fired, but kept a steady advance. The nature of the ground war in our favour so far, for it was so soft that when a bullet or shell struck the ground it stuck there. The Afghans had Snider rifles and twenty-eight field guns, and were estimated on this occasion at 20,000 men. General Roberts' force did not number more than 5,000 men. A, E and F companies of the "Gordons" were the first to engage with the enemy under the command of Major George Stewart White (later Sir George S. White, V. C, K. C. B.), I was in command here of No. 3 section of "F" company.

We had 100 rounds apiece when we started, but although I had some ten rounds left, I cannot for the life of me tell you what took place on the right or left during the advance across the plains. By this time the whole Afghan army was holding the hills of Charasia; we had driven in their outposts. We were now at the bottom of the hills, with plenty of cover, and our six guns pelted at them as we advanced. On our left were the gallant Seventy-Twa and the "wee" Ghourkas.

When we got within 300 or 400 yards of their first entrenchments the whole line was ordered to lie down. The supports and reserves were now pushing hard up to reinforce the fighting line; and most of the enemy's fire now was directed against them.

As soon as General Roberts noticed this, he asked Major White of the 92nd, to try and take those guns. Major White told the *aide* camp to tell General Roberts that he shall have every one of them before the supports came up.

Major White immediately put himself in front of the line, and, shouting with all his might, "Follow me, Highlanders, and make dear auld Scotland ring with cheers this day! Follow me! Come on!" These words we cheered to the echo, and all were most anxious to see the top of the hills. During the advance up the hillside we had very good cover, but the Afghans met us half way, and for a while made several gaps in our ranks. However, we soon got the distance, and made terrible havoc among them. We never lost an inch of ground, though the Afghans fought very bravely.

Meantime Major White spied a weak point, and no sooner did he see young Burness fall than he took his rifle and am-munition, and, still away in front of us all, took a shot now and then with telling effect. About two p.m., having fought our way almost to the mouth of the guns, with one ringing cheer we made a dash on them, and in a few minutes they were ours. Only one man stood to receive us, an old man about eighty years of age who threw stones at us, and struck Major White on the arm. This man, who was commanding the artillery of the Afghan army, was deprived of his sword and sent about his business. We took several prisoners, but let them all go, because we could not spare men to guard them, and our supplies were small. Three different positions were taken in the same manner, Major White displaying the greatest acts of bravery, and showing a grand example to all.

It was on this occasion that Colour-Sergeant Hector Mac-donald, of the 92nd, took two guns with his half company, and was promoted to lieutenant or his gallant conduct. Before six p.m. we had the whole Afghan Army in full retreat, having been engaged for fully twelve hours. That night we bivouacked on the ground we had taken; on the following morning the dead were buried. The 92nd had two killed and six wounded; the

72nd had seven killed and thirty wounded; the Gourkhas and 23rd Pioneers lost some forty men; altogether about 148 were killed or wounded of our force. The Afghans loss was said to be 1500. They had a great number of horses killed. On the morning of the seventh we continued the pursuit, marching round from one hill to another.

On the afternoon of the eighth we found them, strongly posted, in front of the Bala Hassar (King's Palace.) They had several guns, and commenced firing as soon as they saw us. It was now too late to give them battle, so we took up a position, and kept them in check till the morning, when a general advance was to be made. But during the night they bolted and left the city to our mercy, which we took without hardly firing a shot. From the morning of the sixth till the morning of the ninth we did not receive any food, and when we got the flour to make our bread many of us ate the dough, not having the patience to wait till it was baked on the griddles. We had plenty of water, however, but for all that I never knew what hunger was till then. After the city surrendered and the British flag hoisted, we were soon into our bell tents, and had a good round meal of Afghan mutton, and talked loud and long of our first battle.

CHAPTER 8

Retribution in Cabul

After the surrender of the city, the *ameer*, Yakoob Khan, was immediately arrested and sent down to India under a strong escort. All the treasure and everything of any value was seized and put apart as prize money for General Roberts and his army. The estimated value was put down at a little over a million pounds, but as yet not a cent of this money has been given to those who took part in the taking of the city of Cabul.

On the 12th of October, six days after the Battle of Charasia, the whole army marched through the city with fixed bayonets, bands playing and colours flying; afterwards a proclamation I was read to the Afghans to the effect that any person found with arms was liable to be shot.

On the 13th of October over one hundred were arrested and accused of taking part in the massacre of Major Cavagnari and his escort, including Lieutenant Hamilton. Surgeons Jenkins and Kelly, the first men found guilty were the "*khut walla*" or mayor, and his secretary; they were both hung. From this time up to the end of November three and four and sometimes as many as twenty were hung every day; they were all hung with silk ropes. In all eighty-three men suffered death.

After all this, the city people came to feel the strong arm of the invader, and came to our camp with their goods, which always had a ready sale, and sure of their money. They thought for a long time that if they came with goods to our camp that the soldiers would kill them and steal their goods; that is the way the

Afghan does if he is the conqueror; and they were astonished at our generosity and civility towards them. During the trial of the political prisoners there was a colonel of the Afghan Army held to give evidence against them. This officer was badly wounded on the right foot at the Battle of Charasia. He was kept prisoner in the 92nd quarter guard tent; at night he had to be handcuffed to the tent pole.

In this manner the poor fellow could not sleep. I was the sergeant in command of this guard one cold night; and as the sentries were relieved they had to see that he was secure to the tent pole; about 10:30 p.m. rounds had come and gone, and from the time I tied him up he never closed an eye, he could only lay on one side, and sometimes his wound was tramped on by some of the guard moving about in the dark; I felt very much for him, and I took the risk of untying him so as he could have a chance to sleep. As soon as I did so he caressed me in the most affectionate manner. Shortly afterwards he was set at liberty, and one day while fishing in the Cabul River this same colonel with about forty followers saw me taking in a large fish which drew their attention.

As soon as this Afghan officer recognized me he at once dismounted his horse and shook hands and introduced me as I thought, to his followers. I did not understand what he said to me or those with him, but there was soon a person on the spot to act as interpreter; he wished to present me with a splendid charger, with an invitation to visit his residence in Ghiznee. This I could not accept and when told the reason, he said he would go and see General Roberts about it, "But if you do that," said I to the interpreter, "he would ask why you are treating the sergeant and if he came to know it was for what you tell me, the sergeant would be punished." He seemed much disappointed at not having his wish, so after much caressing and shaking of hands he parted from me and I saw him no more. A few weeks after this I was in charge of the commissariat guard in the Afghan barracks of Shapore; here all grain, feed, etc., were stored for the use of the army.

I was not long on guard, when a prisoner was given in my charge; the prisoner was a "Hazarra," a race of people in Afghanistan so like each other that a European or any stranger to them, can hardly tell the one from the other. During my stay in Cabul these people did all the work about the grain: and this man while working around stole Sergeant Hunt's boots. He caught him in the act; so he was put in charge of the guard, and I put him close by the sentry and as it was cold I covered him over with sheepskins, that were for the use of the guard in very cold weather. At 5 a.m. next day I posted the sentries, and the first question the new sentry asked of the old one was "Is your prisoner there?"

"Of course he is?"

"I want to see him before I take over this post."

I immediately went over and lifted skins but there was no prisoner? Private Lamond, the old sentry, on seeing how matters were, said, "Give us a chance, sergeant, I know the man and I'll catch him coming to work at six o'clock." I gave him a chance and kept him on sentry, for they had all to pass by our gate. As soon as they commenced to come, Lamond made a rush in among the crowd, like a shepherd after a sheep, and as he caught him shouted, "I have him, sergeant, here he is!" and none of us could say that he was mistaken. On being arrested the poor fellow could not understand what he had done, and we soon found out that Lamond had the "wrang soo by the lug."

CHAPTER 9

Surrounded

In the early part of December the whole of General Robert's army was in the cantonments of Sherpore: and here all preparations were made in the way of defence and providing supplies for the winter. Every day convoys were sent out, and in some quarters the Afghan farmers would not sell; and in the valley of Maidan, about 18 miles from the city of Cabul, they refused to sell anything in the way of food. Not that they would be short themselves, but that we were *infidels*; this was one of their reasons, but we soon found out to our cost that such was not altogether the case, for our spies brought in word that a large army was to muster here and make an attack, and retake the city from us if we made any more demand for provisions, but General Roberts and his splendid staff knew what that threat meant.

So on the 9th December he sent out the 92nd Highlanders with three mountain guns and four companies of the 23rd Pioneers, but kept the main body of his army in Sherpore, which held full command of the city. Our force which went to Maiden numbered about 1,000. Instead of going right into the valley we took them in flank. This was on the morning of the 10th, and about 8 a.m. we gave them battle, and in a few hours routed them. The first village we entered we captured a lot of horses, camels, etc., but we witnessed a very sad sight.

It was a young girl about 18 years of age lying in the centre of the room with arms and legs cut off. She was still living when we entered, and Captain McCallum ordered Sergeant McFadyen, (later Lieutenant, Govan Police) to put her out of pain by the bayonet. This the sergeant refused to do, saying that he had not got the heart to do it, although death would certainly be welcome to her, but before many minutes after she expired, after partaking of some brandy out of Sergeant Nichol's flask. Her own people did this to her because she would not go with them. On the following day we were completely surrounded, and it was signalled at Cabul that they were hard pressed, and that two of our guns were taken.

The Afghans had us now in a trap; and the news of two of our guns being taken looked pretty bad. But we had the bravest of leaders, and that if we had to die we made up our minds that even although they were ten to one we would die hard. Our Brigadier at once decided to first cut our way through them, and retire to Cabul. We were twelve miles from the city. We attacked them in extended order in echelon, and so rapid was our attack that we were on them before they knew, and killed about 300 of them, capturing many standards.

At this affair Jock Sharp from Glasgow was severely wounded on the shoulder. The Rev. Mr. Manson, our minister, seeing Jock fall ran to his assistance. Jock looked up at Mr. Manson's face and as soon as he saw who was beside him he shouted out, "Dinna pray the noo, sir, bring me a *dhooley*, bring me a *dhooley* (a stretcher)." After forcing our way through them, they were rallying quickly, but we had now a clear road to Cabul, and in a few moments we were in full retreat. But we no sooner started than they were at our heels. This was about 11 a.m., and a hard battle commenced. As they were twenty to one our Brigadier ordered the "Gordon's" to cover the retreat for we were not strong enough to give them battle. Meantime they were pelting away at us on both flanks, and in our rear.

We were all in extended order and commenced to retire by alternate half companies, firing volleys, this we continued for ten consecutive hours, doing them terrible harm, holding them at bay whenever they made any rush. This retreat was the admiration of the war correspondent. The "Gordons," although performing the hardest task in this affair, lost very few men. It was late when we arrived in Cabul, and our comrades were glad to see us, for they had had very hard fighting, also, and our excellent countryman, General MacPherson with the Seventy-twa had recaptured our two guns. I should have said that darkness brought our fighting to an end. I think it was about 10 p.m. when we reached Cabul, and then the whole of General Roberts' army retired into Sherpore for the night.

Tired and footsore, few were off duty that night, for it took nearly the whole of our force for outpost duty, picquets, etc. On the morning of the 13th December, the sound of the pibroch once more told us that the lads wi' the kilts were wanted. Twenty minutes after the pipers had played "Johnny Cope," the 92nd were well on their way to meet the foe with our gallant band of pipers playing the "Cock o' the North." We had not gone one mile when a halt was made. General Roberts after taking a good look at us, ordered that we should take off our rolled greatcoats. This was at once done, and as we moved along we saw our brave gunners getting their field guns into action.

Now we could see the whole Afghan army holding all the hills round the city. At this time the 92nd was in quarter column. In looking at the mass of men in our front whom we were to attack, made many of us feel like that few of us would have a chance to come back, but as we advanced to the attack with our splendid gunners making every shell tell, firing over our heads into them, all such thoughts turned the other way. Gallant White led the advance as usual. So now the great Battle of Takht-i-shah begins where the "Gordons" won two Victoria Crosses and two distinguished medals.

CHAPTER 10

Takht-i-shah

After the command was given for the attack, G and H company of the 92nd were ordered to cover the guns. All the others of the "Gordons" under Major White led the advance across the plains under a terrible fire; but luck was with the Highlanders again, for the ground was so soft that no ball or bullet could ricochet. The first hit, however, was one of our dogs, which was barking and running far away in front of the fighting line. It was most comical to see the poor brute limping on three legs and in full retreat. He was soon in the hands of the ambulance corps, who dressed the wound. Our advance was most rapid, and we (the infantry) did not fire a shot until we got about 600 yards from the enemy. But during this time our splendid gunners were making every shell tell a tale.

On we went, only stopping now and then to fire and take up our dressing. When we got to the bottom of the hill we lay down for a few minutes to have a breath. Major White now dismounted and drew his claymore and revolver. Placing himself in front of the whole line he cried out, "Highlanders, fix bayonets; forward; be steady, keep your dressing!" Just behind us were Colonel Vaughan, of the London *Times*; Mr. Cameron of the *Standard*, and Melton Prior of the *Illustrated London News*, and others. Steadily along we went up the steep hillside. We had not gone 200 yards when we were met by the enemy who seemed anxious to close with us.

They had not long to wait, however, for we were soon in

among them. They fought like tigers, some throwing down their rifles and fighting with their swords, when too close. This hand to hand struggle lasted about ten minutes, and as I pen this my Highland blood leaps in my veins with pride, when I think of the acts of bravery performed by our gallant countrymen on this occasion. In this our first bayonet encounter about twenty of the "Gordons" fell. Still the advance continued up the hill, and we knew by the amount of shot and shell passing over our heads that there were thousands of the enemy waiting to give us a warm reception. Colour-Sergeant James Drummond and Lieutenant Forbes of the 92nd were the first to mount the hill-top. They were almost cut to pieces, but not before they had slain quite a number.

Meantime the whole line was pressing forward under a terrible fire; on the extreme right of the kilted line was Lieutenant Cunningham pressing the Afghans out of every corner, but just as he got to the top of the hill, he was met by thousands, who caused the Highlanders to waver. As soon as Lieutenant Cunningham saw some of his men give way, he rushed in front of his company and cried out, "For God's sake, Highlanders, remember your country; stand with me and fight to the last. Down on the knee, Scots, and give them snuff." Our brave lieutenant had hardly finished his encouraging words when all were down on the knee, pouring volley after volley into them. Presently the voice of gallant White was heard to say. "The bayonet, Highlanders! the bayonet!" By this time the Afghans were wavering on every side. The pipers were soon in their places, and with one terrible yell we were over the rocks and at them.

In this engagement which lasted about five hours, forty-five of the 92nd were wounded and three killed. Lieutenant Grant, from Speyside, had the top brais of his sporran knocked out of shape with a rifle bullet; Corporal McLennan from Dingwall, was hit on his tunic button, the bullet went round his back, made the button as flat as a sixpence, and a black mark round his body like a horse whip; Jock Young and Johnnie Boyd, both from Hawick, had their helmets riddled with bullets; Donald

Williamson, from Clachnacuddin, had his kilt and haversack cut in many places; Drummer Middleton, from Aberdeen, had his claymore broken, but captured a revolver and sword from the enemy; in fact nearly every man in the regiment had some narrow shave; the writer was slightly cut on the left hand while defending Private McLeod. After putting them to rout, our cavalry were after them, but on account of the nature of the ground they were unable to do them any harm.

Many standards and other trophies were taken, and on our way home to camp all these were carried in front of the regiment while our splendid band of pipers struck up "The lads wi' the kilts." As General Roberts and his staff met us, he ordered us to halt. He then addressed us in the most enthusiastic manner, saying he was glad to see so many gentlemen representing the London press, who have seen with their own eyes the kind of stuff of which we are made. General Roberts and his staff saw the whole affair, and he asked for the names of officers, non-commissioned officers and men who had specially distinguished themselves on this occasion. Major White said that all had done their duty, and if he recommended one he would do the same to all.

Nevertheless Colonel Brownlow of the 72nd Highlanders reported the conduct of Sergeant Jno. McLaren and Corporal McKay of the 92nd, and each received the distinguished conduct medal. Major White and Lieutenant Cunningham both won the Victoria Cross for repeated acts of bravery, and Sergeants Cox and Macdonald, of the 72nd were each awarded the distinguished conduct medal and clasp for the gallant way they saved the life of Captain Cook, of the Gourkhas, who was severely wounded. Captain Cook was a native of Ross-shire. He died, poor fellow, the day after, and, as our brave general said, a finer soldier never drew a sword.

About 7 p.m. our camp fires were in full blast, and after supper and partaking of our grog, we sang round our fires such songs as had a long chorus, such as "Ancient Stirling," and others, and felt as happy as could be. We were always in the best of spirits, no matter what hardships or fighting.

On Sunday, the 14th December, the 72nd with some Gour-khas and two companies of the 92nd were told off to clear the Asmi Heights where the remnants of the army of the 13th were said to be gathering. About two hours after they had gone, they signalled for reinforcements, saying that they were hard pressed and that Captain Gordon of the 92nd was badly wounded. In a short time the pibroch sounded once more to arms, and putting some bread in our haversacks and water in our bottles we were off to meet the foe.

CHAPTER 11

In the Trenches

By the time we were outside camp some of the 9th Lancers came galloping past us, and one of their officers told us that the enemy had received large reinforcements from Herat and other places, and that two of the mule battery guns were taken. We were soon in extended order and could plainly see the enemy in swarms all over the Asmi Heights, and our men pelting at them. About two o'clock a general retreat was ordered, and the 92nd Highlanders were ordered to cover it. After all our men got safely off the hill, all made for the cantonments of Sherpore, which we had strongly entrenched. This retreat was the finest sight I ever saw.

Away on the extreme left were the gallant "Seventy-twa," retiring in splendid order, as were also the famous Gourkhas, firing into them by alternate companies. On each flank were our cavalry ready and anxious for a dive at them should they threaten to flank us. In the centre of the whole were the 92nd retiring slowly and firing by sections, and over all our heads were our artillery firing shell into them. Here and there you could see two or three men carrying a wounded comrade and mules carrying the dead, mounted officers rushing here and there giving orders and encouraging words to the men.

The retreat was kept up till we came within a few hundred yards of our trenches. Here a stand was made, and as soon as the enemy saw this they retired and took possession of the city. On this Sabbath morning about twenty of the 72nd were killed and some forty wounded. Captain Gordon of the 92nd was shot through the left lung. Corporal Sellar of the 72nd won the Victoria Cross, and the Rev. Mr. Adams also won the Victoria Cross for saving the life of a boy of the 9th Lancers. In the retreat the boy's horse was shot under him, and as the horse fell the trumpeter was badly hurt, and could not follow up. In a few moments the Afghans would be at him, and the brave minister, knowing this, galloped back to where the poor boy lay, at once dismounted, put the lad on his horse, then mounted beside him and made his way through a storm of bullets safe to the main body.

On all sides the cry was, "Bravo, Mr. Adams!" The Rev. Mr. Adams was the English Church minister of the army. I believe he is the first and only minister who wears this great honour. Corporal Sellar, a native of Huntly in Aberdeenshire, won his Victoria Cross for one of the most daring acts in the whole campaign. When moving up the slopes of the Asmi Heights, the enemy were posted in small forts or *sunghas*, with as many as ten to twenty men in each. Into one of these Corporal Sellar rushed single-handed and bayoneted them right and left; and Corporal Calder of the 92nd, and some others, were just in time to save him from a terrible death, for he was cut in all directions.

As Corporal Calder entered, he had no room to use the bayonet; he threw his rifle to one side and let the first fellow have it with the bare fists, in true British style, but had his hands cut badly while parrying the blows of the Afghan knives; and Sergeant John McLaren, a powerful Highlander from the braes o' Balquhidder, also of the 92nd, had his sword bayonet almost bent in two while pitching an Afghan out of the *sungha* where Corporal Sellar was. Drummer Girvan of the 72nd, a fine soldier from Ayrshire, was killed with a stone by an Afghan when trying to retake the guns.

About six p.m., firing on both sides ceased, and before we had time to think of anything, each regiment had to send in returns showing the number of men fit for duty, and by eight o'clock same night it was known that there were only 4,276 men all told; and that the Afghan army, which was now in possession of the city had, according to the *Times* correspondent, some 70,000 men. Everything was now pushed with the greatest haste for our defence, and by nine o'clock same eight every regiment knew their place. The cantonments of Sherpore are about two miles in circumference; nearly the half consists of a mud wall about twenty feet high, so that a few outposts were sufficient to guard that quarter, but the other part had to be well trenched. The 92nd were posted at the Gorge, as it was called, and certainly the weakest point.

I should have mentioned in the early part of my story that we captured all the guns the Afghans had, in all 281, of all sizes. Most of these were taken out of the magazine in the Bala Hassar, and on the 16th Oct. some person blew the whole magazine up. There was a guard of the Gourkhas on at the time of the explosion, twelve men, a sergeant and a corporal They were all blown to pieces, together with a large amount of treasure. A private of the 67th Regiment was signalling at the time some 400 yards from the place, a long plank struck him and almost cut him in two. It took two days to burn out, and the damage done to the city was very great.

To return to the trenches. Well, in front of our trench we had trees laying flat with all their branches on, and wire netted in all sorts of shape, so that it was impossible for large bodies to come up in good formation. For ten consecutive days and nights we lay in these trenches, and our orders were, no man to fire until the enemy came within eighty yards of us. It must be remembered that we were now hemmed in on all sides and cut off from all communication. General Gough, who commanded the forces down by Gundamak, signalled on the 18th that reinforcements had been sent to us.

From that day on many an anxious eye looked over their trench to see if help was nigh, but no signs in any direction. During the siege the enemy never ceased firing from daylight till dark, and every day horses, camels, dogs and many of our force ware killed. We hardly ever fired, except now and then a few young officers would go out for a few flying shots at them.

On the seventh day it was known that there were only about 200 rounds per man to the fore, and no man was allowed to fire a shot except ordered to do so. We had many spies out every night, but very few ever came back. Every day we captured some of their spies, who were at once shot. Every day the enemy were receiving reinforcements, and the plans of their attack were well known to all of us. All the captured guns were placed in a square formation in the centre of our entrenchments. And here we were all to rush to if they forced us out of the trenches, and here we were to do or die, for the Afghan gives no quarter, and this we all knew full well.

The ninth day has come, still no help yet. There was much snow on the ground at the time, and this prevented them very much. We never had our clothes off day or night, and very seldom our belts; still we were as happy as the day was long, and many a good song and story were gone over during these trying and anxious times.

The tenth day has come, and a few of the many spies have just come in, informing us that our reinforcements are in sight, and that a council of war has been held by the enemy and they are to make a grand attack on us before they will be able to arrive. The attack will take place at daybreak by one army coming by the north front, the other by the east and west fronts; and the signal for attack was the lighting of a large fire on the Asmi Heights; and all their cavalry was to force the Commissariat Gate and cut us up as we retired from our trenches. Such were the plans of the Afghans, to repeat the cruel affair of 1842, for there were many in their ranks at this time who had taken part in that sad affair. Every man of our force knew these facts, and all made up their minds that if they had to die they would do so like their fathers before them, with their faces to the foe.

CHAPTER 12

The City Retaken

By 3 a.m. on the 23rd of December, every man (white and black) knew full well that they were to fight against terrible odds, and you could hear the whisper along the trenches among the "Gordons," "Let every volley tell a tale," and "Do or die." There were about six inches of snow on the ground but it was not very cold. All was quiet, but every eye was cast on our gallant general, who was to tell us when to strike: "Oh, I wish they would come on!" some soldier would say. Then you could hear among the general's staff, "I wonder how the forlorn hope will come out?" The Hon. John Scott Napier, a son of Lord Napier of Ettrick, had command of the forlorn hope, which consisted of fifty volunteers of the 92nd. These were to hold back the Afghan cavalry and they were to force their way in by the main gate.

Before posting his men Captain Napier told them, "that every man must fight to the last and any man who is not willing to die with me, let him fall out." Every man stood still and their silence meant, as the *Pioneer* has it, "Let us do or die." All men in the hospital who were able to sit on a chair and pull a trigger were placed behind the ramparts with the three ministers in command. Father Brown, a fine old gentlemen, of whom I will have more to say later, Mr. Adams, the English minister, and Mr. Mason, the Scotch, were doing their utmost to keep up the spirits of our wounded and sick comrades. Now and then the priest would shout, "We are sure to win, boys, for it is Jesus Christ against Mahomet; give it to them hot."

Exactly at 5 a.m. the fire was seen on the Asmi Heights, and no sooner did it appear than a rocket went right over our heads. This was the signal for the attack on us. What an anxious moment that was! Here we were, down low in our trenches, like cats waiting to dash at their prey; not even a whisper, until they were about eighty yards from us. Meantime the long black mass of men came steadily along beating their drums, and shouting "*Allah! Allah!*" (God! God!)

"Now, Highlanders," cried Col. Macgregor, chief of the staff, "give them it hot." We were just at the "present," when this fine officer spoke these words. The first volley was not a good one, but the next was, to say the least, superb, in short, it made a gate right through them. After firing four splendid volleys, the order came along the line, "independent firing." The sound of our musketry then was terrible, and we mowed them down as soon as they came up. Not even the sound of the pipers could be heard, the noise was so great. This great roll of musketry continued for about twenty minutes, or more. Meantime our cavalry were ready to make the dash on them, as soon as we got them on the run. But many had taken up cover, and lay firing into us. As soon as this was noticed the whole line was ordered to charge, and with Highlanders yelling and the others cheering, we were over the trenches and at them.

They were taken so suddenly that they bolted in wild confusion. We now stood resting on our arms, watching our cavalry cutting at them right and left, and putting the finishing stroke to the investment of Sherpore. The most remarkable thing of this engagement, which lasted about one hour, was the few killed and wounded—there was not forty men of the whole force. Colonel Gough was thrown off his horse by a rifle bullet, but as he had a coat of mail on, he was not killed. Major White's horse was shot through the ear. A *sepoy* of the 28th Punjab Infantry had his left ear blown off by his rear-rank man.

Our cavalry were back by eleven a. m., and what a sight! They were covered with blood and mud; a great number without helmets and lances; some without horses, thus showing that they had done some terrible destruction. The city again fell into our hands, and we were once more the conquerors. What a happy crowd we were now. All communications were now open and in a few days our convoys would be up with our provisions. I must not forget to tell you that from the 10th of November to the 25th of December, we were without any tobacco, and to the soldier on duty this is a great want. During these trying times, we smoked anything that could make "*reek*," such as old rags, leaves of trees, straw mixed with tea; and matches, too, were worth their weight in gold; but we made match-paper out of powder, and fell back on the steel and flint.

We had plenty of food, however, and clothing, for the ladies in India sent us plenty of warm socks, etc., etc. After this grand victory the Afghans commenced to see that there was no hope or chance fighting against us. Their armies wore completely broken; all their guns were taken, and thousands of rifles were destroyed and buried—in short, they were subdued. Such was the opinion expressed in the Indian press, but they were all sadly mistaken. For, as the people of the city told us, as soon as they got their crops in, they would muster again; but not in this quarter; and as I go along with my story we will see how true this comes out.

Snow is still on the ground, and all the fighting is over, so far as we know. The two Highland regiments put their heads together, and send a challenge to our English and Irish comrades for a snow battle. Major Douglas and Captain Napier of the 92nd, are to command the Scottish army; Captains Murray and Munro, of the 72nd, also taking a leading part. Forts are built and trenches, etc., on the Bahmara Heights. At 9 a.m. sharp the pibroch sounded for the sons of Caledonia to rally and fight the Battle of Bannockburn over again; and in my next I will tell you how many were slain.

Chapter 13

"The Battle of Bannockburn"

I should have mentioned in the last chapter that Captain, the Hon. John Scott Napier, and his gallant band, which composed the forlorn hope, were sadly disappointed for they never had to fire a shot. But why? Because the Afghan leader knew that night that fifty determined *feringie gazies* (foreign warriors) swore to die before they would let their cavalry pass the gate. "*Feringie Gazie*" was the name the Afghans gave the kilted Highlanders, and it may be interesting to note that the Gordon Highlanders were the only regiment who had not a man murdered on the streets of Cabul or Kandahar. The Afghans were very fond of the Highland dress, and in the field of battle they shunned us as much as they could, especially when they could see the glitter of our sporrans in the sunshine as we advanced on them to the attack.

But why were the Afghans so fond of the Highland dress? In 1859, when Ameer Sher Ali, king of Afghanistan, came down to India, the 92nd Highlanders were reviewed in front of him, and he was so much amazed at the fine appearance of the regiment that he wanted to buy it there and then. When the viceroy told him that such a thing was impossible he was much disappointed; but before he left India he gave orders to have 10,000 kilts and Highland tunics made for his army with 92nd buttons on them. On his return to Afghanistan he composed ten kilted regiments, and they were the pick of the Afghan army.

After the taking of Cabul more than a thousand of these kilts and tunics fell into our hands, and it seemed so odd to see our own buttons on them. These tunics and kilts were given to our camp-followers, and they did grand service to them during the winter; but what a sight they were! Fancy a black man with a kilt trailing down to his heels and the tunic outside in and minus the buttons. And should this catch the eye of anyone who were there to see, it will bring back many a hearty laugh. So much for Sher Ali's kilted men. But what about the forlorn hope! Well, Captain Napier was promoted major, but nothing was done for the gallant fellows who had sworn to die with their gallant captain. However there was no room for complaint as their services were not put to the test; but as every Briton knows they do funny things in the army.

After all the fighting and worry we had a good rest; and the challenge to fight our English and Irish comrades in a snow battle was at once accepted. None of the *sepoys* or Ghoorkas would join, but a great number of the officers of these corps took part, the Scotch officers coming to our side and the others to the English side. The pipes of the Scottish army sounded the gathering of the clans about 9.30 a.m., each man armed with two haversacks to carry the snowballs. Nearly all the officers were mounted. After the corps, *viz.*: 72nd and 92nd, were told off in half companies and sections, Major Douglas of the 92nd gave the command. "The brigade will form for attack." The English army was posted in a range of low hills in the Cantonments of Sherpore, and had forts built of snow dotted all over the hill side. We, the Scottish army, had all kinds of flags that we had captured, but we had the Royal Standard of Scotland with another behind it, with an awful size of a thistle on it and the following words:

McNeil of the islands,
And Moy of the lake,
For honour, for freedom,
For vengeance awake!

Of course all this was just a kind of burlesque. At 10 a.m. we were advancing in splendid order to the attack, and the shouts, cheering, etc., was something awful. Just fancy about two thousand sons of auld Scotia out for a day's fun! No harm could be done to the enemy until we came just to throwing distance, but as soon as we came about to embrace our Sassenach friends, the shower of snowballs came on us like hailstones, but on we went reserving our ammunition till we closed with them. Then! Oh then! the yells and shouts. Down went the forts in rapid succession, and it was here we could see after closing with them where the power of the Highlanders was.

After gaining the top of the hill where they had gathered to make the last stand, our Sassenach friends became somewhat angry. Here Lieutenants McBain, Grant and Stewart, of the 92nd, seeing Captains Stewart. McKenzie and Chisholm of the 9th Lancers fighting hard against us, rushed at them, shouting "Down with the traitors! Down with them!" The struggle continued for nearly two hours, and it was admitted on all sides that the Highlanders had it all their own way. General Roberts and his staff witnessed the whole affair, and enjoyed themselves so much that they remarked that they felt proud of the Highland brigade. I have seen many a snow battle in my Highland home but never such a one as this. Just think of it, nearly 2,000 a side, all under officers, where no man could or would dare to disobey an order, fighting with snowballs.

By 12.30 p.m. the Battle of Bannockburn was fought and won, but there was not one killed of either army, but there were hundreds wounded and the worst of all was Lieutenant McBlain, who had two blue eyes, Captain Douglas, Lieutenant Bethune and Colour-Sergeant W. Fraser were cut in several parts of the face. Captain Murray, of the 2nd, and Lieutenant Drummond were cut badly also; this was caused by our foes throwing ice and stones at us, but in fairness to all, one was as bad as the other on that score. Nevertheless Scotland won the day, and just as the first bugle had sounded for dinner we were on the march back to camp with our splendid band playing that fine march "Scotland the Brave."

In concluding this chapter it may be interesting to note the corps composing the English army, *viz.*: Artillery about 76 men, 9th Lancers about 250 men, 9th Regt. (or better known as the 9th Holy Boys) about 500 men, 67th Hampshire Regt. about 600 men, officers of the Indian army about 20, making a total of nearly 1,500. The Gordons were fully 600 strong, the 72nd Highlanders were about the same, and the other Scots of the army brought up our total to about 1,300 men. During the battle the Afghans thought we were fighting and quarrelling among ourselves and as I go on with my story it will be seen how sadly they were disappointed.

CHAPTER 14

Fort Abraham

After the snow had cleared away all the villages or houses sur-rounding the cantonments of Sherpore were pulled down and levelled to the ground. The reason of this was that during the investment those who lived in them gave shelter and assisted the Afghan army in doing all the harm they could to us. It may be interesting to note that there are no single houses in Afghanistan except in cities. The reason they are called villages is because there are so many families in them. These villages are built of clay and all walled in, there being only" one gate on each, with a turret at each corner. The oldest men who are unable to work keep watch all night, and that is all they do.

In the city of Cabul there are three gates, and all must be in at a certain hour, and it is just the same in the villages. It is a pretty sight to see the Afghans marching home in groups to their respective homes as their tattoo draws nigh. During the investment these villages were filled with marksmen who kept un a continual fire from daylight till dark; and as our artillery ammunition wan running short, we only fired into them when there was a good chance.

After the destruction of the villages we built splendid forts and roads. Each fort had a name and the finest of them all was called Fort Abraham, situated on the banks of the Cabul River. When we entered Cabul first it was full of dirt and filth; so dirty indeed that it would make you sick. Early in March General Roberts made the people of the city form a scavenger corps, just like what we have in our towns in Scotland. Sanitary officers from our army were appointed to teach them and to see the work done. The Afghans did not like this at first, but they soon began to see the good it did them. They were much astonished at the fine roads we made, a thing hardly known in that country. All the roads that ever I saw in the country were camel tracks.

It is now April, and the Afghans are busy preparing their farms and gardens. And we are mostly engaged surveying all the country for miles around. Fresh rumours come from the city every day that armies are coming to destroy us like they did our forefathers in 1842. Perhaps it may not be out of my story to here mention in a brief manner the sad affair of 1842, and thus give my readers an idea of what kind of people the Afghans are. The Afghans have sadly deteriorated in character within the present century. Take, for example, their atrocious conduct in the Persian war.

On that occasion the Afghan ruler invited 300 of the Persian nobles to a grand feast, and then, when they were in the midst of enjoyment, happy in the thought that they were now at peace, and on friendly terms with a powerful neighbour, they were, in the most treacherous and cowardly manner, all cruelly massacred. But this was not all. As if the monster's tigerish taste for blood had been only whetted, he gave orders for the slaughter of some 3,000 of the Persian guards, who had also been invited to a friendly meeting with his own adherents . When Elphinstone's army began that sad retreat from Cabul, which should never have taken place, and which could only end in disaster, many noble examples of heroic suffering and undaunted courage were given; but when met by the cold-blooded, perfidious cunning of the Afghans, they were of little avail.

Particularly was this the case with four officers who were fellow-companions in this retreat. After many a weary mile, they had halted to rest within a few miles of Jellalabad. To their surprise a party of Afghans approached them making signs that they were friends, and carrying them supplies of food, which they appeared anxious to give them. To the famishing young officers this appeared like a miraculous intervention to save their lives. Was it any wonder if they found themselves taking blame for thinking that there was no good left in an Afghan, and that they would think better of them in future? Alas! For them, poor fellows, there was to be no future; for scarcely had they began to satisfy their craving hunger, when they were set upon by these veritable wolves in sheep's clothing and literally cut to pieces. Can we be blamed then for taking every precaution? Every one of us, Gael and Saxon, swore in our hearts, that rather than fall into the hands of such a foe we would die at our posts first.

CHAPTER 15

The Chilductean Valley

Ending up in my last chapter about the treacherous nature of the Afghan, it will be interesting to include here one incident that came under my own observation. A sergeant of the 12th Suffolk Regiment, while out with some others for a day's sport among the hills near Gundamuk, lost his chums, and on his way to camp called into a village for a drink of water. When in the act of drinking the water, a swarm of Afghans rushed at him and bound him hand and foot. After doing this with ropes, they took all his teeth out, then the nails off his hands and feet, and after that they cut him open and allowed the poor fellow to die in the greatest agony. I could give many such incidents of their cruel nature, some indeed not fit for publication.

However, to pass over these sad things, let me give a picture of the Afghans at home. Amongst the better classes great pride is taken in their origin and descent, their native historians claiming that they come from the Jews, who were taken captive by the Babylonians and brought to the range of country between Herat and Cabul. The male population are generally of swarthy colour, and possessed of sinewy, lithe, and active bodies. The females are generally of fair complexion, handsome, and attractive. Their costume consists, when at home, of a loose skirt like those worn by the men, but longer, and made of finer material. When they appear in public they are completely covered by a long veil, having holes for the eyes and mouth.

The unmarried women wear their hair hanging loose and

are generally dressed in white trousers. Women occupy a low position in the social scale, and are bartered and purchased like common merchandise. A plurality of wives is the custom among the Afghans, the number for one husband generally being four. The men are fond of smoking, particularly a mixture called *gun-jah*, which brings on a kind of intoxication. The greatest honour an Afghan can pay to a white man is to bring him to his house and there unveil his ladies in front of him.

It is now April and the weather is lovely, just cold enough to sleep well at night and we have all the necessaries of this life at hand. Peace reigns on all sides; each regiment has squads of men here and there with picks and shovels making roads, and the Government of India is considering who they will make King of Afghanistan, when one fine morning we were informed that a great battle was fought about twenty miles from us, by General Sir Donald Martin Stewart, who was marching from Candahar to join General Sir F. Roberts at Cabul, with an army of 7,000 men.

This army was composed of 2nd 60th Rifles, 59th Regiment and a 40 pound elephant battery, together with a battery of Royal Horse Artillery, and the other portion of *sepoys* and Gourkhas. At place called Ahmed Khel they were attacked by some 20,000 Afghans, and after one hour's hard fighting the Afghans were defeated with great slaughter. The day after this battle, some three companies of the 92nd, 23rd Pioneers and Gourkhas were sent out to the valley of Charasia, to watch the movements of the Afghan army, which Sir Donald Martin Stewart defeated a few days before. This small force, some 900 men in all, was under command of Colonel Jenkins of the Guides Cavalry.

On Sunday morning. 25th April, 1880, just as we were falling in for divine service, an A.D.C. came galloping up to our colonel, and cried out so loud that every man could hear him, *viz.*: "Colonel Jenkins is completely surrounded and General Roberts wants you to be ready to march with all haste in fifteen minutes from now. On hearing these words every man of us was off like a shot to our tents, got our 100 rounds of ammunition and a small piece of bread and meat in our haversacks. Inside of ten minutes we were off to join the rest of the brigade, which was to muster at the headquarters tent, and which was now composed of the 72nd and 92nd Highlanders together with the 3rd Gourkhas, 28th Sepoys and two mountain guns.

A great mistake was made here, and it was not noticed till we were some seven miles on our way, where we had the first halt. The 92nd Highlanders were put in front of the column and the gallant "Wee Gourkhas" were in rear; and when we halted they were some two miles behind us. The average height of the Gourkhas is about five feet three inches, and when you compare the stride of a regiment of kilted Highlanders to these little fellows, it is plain to be seen how they could not keep up, especially when it was forced marching; besides a kilted soldier has the full use of his limbs, and it is in cases like this where the superiority of the kilt is shown over the trousers for campaigning.

After the Gourkhas came up they were put in the centre of the column. We were still seven miles from the enemy, and we could plainly hear the roll of musketry, which told us that we could not be there too soon. And sure enough we see the flash from the heliograph, which our signalmen are hurrying to reply. "What's the news, Mac?" a voice from the ranks would say, to which Corporal Macpherson answered, "Seventeen horses of the Guides killed; Highlanders and Pioneers doing splendid, but running short of ammunition. Cannot hold out long."

Another flash, and Mac. comes running up to the column again.

"How is it now, Mac.?"

"Hemmed in on all sides; enemy in full possession of the orchards. As you come up attack them on left flank."

Such news made us feel anxious to get there; and while we Highlanders were pacing over the ground as hard as we could the poor wee Gourkhas had to double to keep up. Brigadier H. T. McPherson, V.C, of Lucknow fame, was in command of our brigade, and as we advanced into the valley of Chilductean and formed for attack, General McPherson came galloping up to the 92nd Highlanders and said, "Now, countrymen, show those Gourkhas the way, for it is the first time they have been under fire."

I should say here that there are five regiments of Gourkhas, the regiment referred to here being the 3rd Gourkhas, one of the regiments that came to reinforce us during the investment of Sherpore. The battle is now in full swing and so far as I am concerned I feel exceedingly proud, for the sight is a grand one, a full description of which I will give to you in my next.

Chapter 16

The Unsung Battle

I think it was about 2 p.m. when we reached Colonel Jenkins' force, thus covering a distance of fully fourteen miles in two hours and a-half, under a hot April sun, and only one halt. As soon as General Macpherson saw how matters were he did not attack on the left flank, but made right for their centre. The ground was favourable for manoeuvring until we got to the gardens. The whole of our force was in position and on the move long before our comrades were aware of the fact. "Wee Mac," (as we Highlanders affectionately called the General) put us into the finest formation I ever saw. Meantime the 72nd Highlanders formed the line of communication between us and Cabul.

The 3rd Gourkhas were in extended order in the centre, the 92nd Highlanders on the extreme right, and the *sepoys* and Pioneers away on the left. As we advanced to the attack, and according to the position the enemy held, we were able to show three fronts, that is to say, right, left, and centre fronts. We moved on like this till we came near the orchards, which were swarming with the enemy, and hundreds of them up on the apple and other trees. These orchards are all surrounded by mud walls, with one or two gates.

The 92nd Highlanders were the first to enter. Lieutenant Hector Macdonald, of the 92nd, I think, was the first officer inside; and it was here where the writer saw the first man fall before his rifle. I was in command of No. 2 section as soon as

Colour-Sergeant Fraser was wounded, and as I rushed in, I ordered Private Abercromby to fire at a man who was just covering us. He fired and missed; the Afghan rushed at us, sword in hand, and as he touched the point of my sword-bayonet my bullet went through his body and he fell at my feet. "Bravo, Sergeant Martin!" cried the men of my section.

Meantime our attention was called to the trees, where, as we advanced, they mostly all went to hide, and we brought them down in dozens, and the sight reminded me of shooting young crows in Culloden wood or at Dun's near Clachnaharry, Yes! it was a sight indeed—fools that they were—trying to find cover up on a tree, where we picked them off as we pleased. In less than two hours we had them in full retreat, and as they ran across the plain many of them would have bitten the dust only for one of their number having on a red coat. He was so conspicuous among the others that all the fire was directed at him. He ran a distance of about 600 yards before he was able to get under cover. It would not be too much to say that fully six thousand rounds was fired at this one man, and he never was touched. This will give my readers an idea of the chances a soldier has in war.

This engagement was called the Battle of Chilductean, and one of the most brilliant of the whole campaign, to say nothing of the marching out and marching back to camp. It was about 9 p.m. when the combined bands of the 72nd and 92nd met us. Just before they joined us we were hardly able to draw one foot after the other, for be it remembered we covered about forty miles that day, but at the first tap of the big drum, and the first note of the "Blue Bonnets Over the Border," sore feet and hunger were forgotten. A ringing cheer went up from front to rear, and many joined in the chorus of this well-known tune, and our Scottish hearts burned with joy when we thought of showering another honour on dear auld Scotia, and that we too were adding glory to the already noble record of Highland soldiers.

The Guides' Cavalry lost heavily in this engagement in men and horses, for they had to stand under a terrible fire for fully three hours. They could not obtain cover of any kind, and could not do any harm to the enemy, for they were all in the gardens, behind the mud walls; but the fire of Captain Macgregor's company of the 92nd Highlandmen was splendid, which saved the Guides a great deal, and when we buried their dead and our own the next day this was plainly to be seen, for more than two-thirds of them were shot through the head. The 92nd Highlanders had three killed and thirteen wounded; 3rd Gourkhas, one killed and four wounded; 23rd Pioneers, three wounded; Guides' Cavalry, eight men killed and nineteen wounded, and about twenty-four horses killed and wounded.

Sergeant Lawson, of the 92nd, while taking a drink of water out of his canteen, had the canteen thrown out of his hand, and a small piece of the bullet lodged in his neck, Jamie, who hails frae Aberdeen, remarked, as the canteen went spinning out of his hand, "Ye might hae waited till I was dun." Tommie Jardine, one of our drummers frae the Borders, was hit while blowing the right wheel on the bugle. Poor Tommie lost the right hand, but he is now a missionary to a mining district in Cornwall, (as at time of first publication), England. Colour-Sergeant Tam Smith, frae the kingdom of Fife, one of the finest soldiers in the regiment, was mortally wounded while leading his half company through the gardens.

The Gordons captured many trophies of war, including many splendid standards, some which can be seen in the officers' and sergeants' mess today. Such was the Battle of Chilductean, acknowledged to be the finest piece of generalship in any of our former battles, and yet I feel sorry to say that no clasp was given for it, thus putting the 3rd Gourkhas out of the campaign with barefooted medal. Why there was no clasp given for this brilliant victory still remains a mystery, but I have heard since I left the army that the clasp given for Cabul included this engagement, and that the 3rd Gourkhas had received three months pay instead.

The army in Cabul at the beginning of May was fully 20,000 men, with about 1,200 horses and twenty-four guns. Sir Donald M. Stewart was in command. In the month of June the 92nd

Highlanders built a kind of a theatre, and produced our own national drama *Rob Roy*, and a kind of burlesque composed by one of the officers of General Roberts' staff entitled *Robinson Crusoe*. In *Rob Roy* the writer took the part of Francis Osbaldistan. This was got up for the widows of the regiment and the whole affair was a grand success. Before the curtain fell in the burlesque we all sang to the air of the Military Guards—

> *There is a jovial Irishman*
> *Whose name I need not tell;*
> *He is just the man for a brilliant dash*
> *And that we know right well,*
> *A better we could not have here,*
> *No matter how they blame;*
> *Old England trusts him, so do we,*
> *And Roberts is his name!*

CHAPTER 17

To the Rescue

Some fine acts of heroism were done by the "Gordons" at
the Battle of Chilductean, and yet none of these were brought
to the notice of the general. The reason of this was that, when
everything had been arranged to send the names of those who
had displayed such acts of bravery on the field, the cry from
Kandahar came for help. At this time General Sir D. M. Stewart
was still in command at Cabul. But before going any further,
I must state that on the 28th July, 1880, General Burrows was
completely defeated by Ayob Khan, at a place called Maywandd
(Maiwand); General Burrows was in command of an army of
some 3,000 men, consisting of the 66th Regiment, R. H. Artillery (six guns), and some *sepoy* Regiments.

In this battle the 66th Regiment lost their colours but not
before some three hundred gallant fellows died around them.
The remnants of General Burrows' army retired to the city of
Kandahar; and with General Primrose's force they were able
to hold Ayob Khan at bay. But their provisions were small and
consequently they could not hold out long. Like all cities in
Asia Kandahar is walled all round with mud. After this defeat of
General Burrows the greatest fears were apprehended for the
army then in the country, which numbered about 55,000 men,
divided as follows: about 20,000 in Cabul; 7,000 between Quet-
ta and Kandahar; about 11,000 between Cabul and the Khyber
Pass; about 7,000 between the Shutargardan and Khurm Valley,
and the other portion doing convoy duty and signalling all over

the country.

As soon as the news reached us, Sir Donald Stewart at once decided to send an army to the rescue of the garrison at Kandahar. He ordered General Roberts to select his own regiments, which was to consist of twelve infantry regiments, three cavalry regiments and eighteen mountain guns. The 72nd and 92nd Highlanders were the first on the list, then came the 2nd-60th Rifles and 9th Lancers, this was the European portion of the army, together with one mountain screw gun battery, the rest were composed of *sepoys*. General Ross was in command of the infantry brigade. Colonel Jenkins was in command of the cavalry and Colonel Sweeney the artillery. The selection was well received in all quarters, and the *Civil and Military Gazette* of the Punjab said that General Roberts had certainly picked the best regiments; looking back at the bravery displayed by these two dashing regiments of Highlanders around Cabul was sufficient proof of this.

On the 9th August, 1880, everything was ready for the now celebrated march to Kandahar. All of the officers made themselves as light as possible, for four or five of them slept in one tent. To move an army of 10,000 men in a country like Afghanistan means that nearly 10,000 camels, mules and elephants are required to carry them on. When we left Cabul we had fully 10,000 beasts of burden and nearly as many camp followers. All our trophies of war had to be left behind, those of the officers' were shipped to India, as were also those of the sergeants' mess; but those of the men had to be left, and some fine things they were. At the Battle of Charasia, Private Colin McRae, a fine soldier, from Clachnacuddin, captured a pure silk banner, killing his man before he could get possession of it; Jock McLeod, another fine fellow, had some fine swords and pistols; and the writer had some fine trophies also.

All there were put into the hands of the 9th Holy Boys, a regiment that never fired a shot in the country. Nearly every man both in the 72nd and 92nd Highlanders had to sacrifice all their hard won things, which we intended to bring to Auld

Scotland, but fate decreed otherwise. On the morning of the 10th August, 1880, the brave army of General Roberts turned the back of their hands to Cabul, the gallant Gordons leading the way, with the bands of the 9th regiment and 59th playing "Will you No Come Back Again." The army that was left with Sir Donald Stewart turned out to a man, mounted the walls of Bala Hissar and cheered us to the echo. The sight was grand, and as we Highlanders responded to the cheer I felt awfully proud, and as I pen those happy scenes I feel the very hairs of my head standing on end, for this was one of the many happy moments of my life in that long and tedious campaign.

The night before we left Cabul, one of our sentries on outpost duty, shot a horse which had strayed from the inside line; he challenged of course, and, as there was no answer, he fired and hit him on the hip; the night was very dark. About this time also. Private John Muir of "B" company, 92nd Highlanders, caused quite a commotion; Muir was a great man for walking in his sleep, and on this night, when all were fast asleep, he was at his old game, and as soon as he got into No. 3 tent, "C" company, he caught hold of Jock Wilson by the throat. Jock who was fast asleep at the time, at once was on his feet, shouting murder, and Muir joining in chorus. Every man was up out of bed long before the alarm sounded. In case of a night attack each regiment forms a cordon round their tents; no firing is allowed the bayonet only to be used. In this manner we formed on hearing the noise of Private Muir, and many the fine laugh we had when a few minutes after we were informed of Johnnie Muir at his old tricks again.

We are now fourteen miles from Cabul, cut away from all communication, and Sir Donald M. Stewart and his staff shake hands with General Roberts and his army and wish us all God speed.

A full description of the celebrated march will be given in my next.

CHAPTER 18

The March to Kandahar

It was not till the 10th August that General Roberts and his brave band got properly started for Kandahar.

Forced or any other marching in India is gone over in stages; that is to say, before you start, it is published in regimental orders the number of miles you have to march each day, and you know exactly the number of days it will take to arrive at your destination. But in this march such was far from being the case. Reveille sounded every day at 12.30 am., and the whole army was on the move by 2 a.m. The advance guard was on the move by 1.20 a.m., out it was sometimes 4 a.m. before the rear guard or flank guards could move on. The reason of this, of course, was according to the nature of the ground, and in the manner the army had to march, so that the marching was continued till man and beast could march no farther that day.

I should say here, however, that on a rapid march like this, camels die in hundreds, and from the day we left Cabul till the day we sighted Kandahar, hundreds were left dead at the road side. The rear guard, which consisted of one infantry regiment, had spare animals to take the burdens of the fallen ones, but some days they had not enough, and the result was that some of the men had to do without tents and other things. It was seldom we ever pitched tents: we spread them on the ground and laid close to each other like sardines in a box. Some days we were 2000 feet above the level of the sea, and other days down to sea level. We crossed five rivers, and it was here again that General

Roberts and his staff saw the superiority of the Highland garb,

In every case the Highlanders were over first. If the river was, say, two or three feet deep it was a general walk across, re-forming at the other side; but if it were breast high we crossed six and eight abreast, locking each other arm in arm. with rifles slung over the shoulder. Big heavy men carried the band and drummer boys on their backs. Before crossing any river, we Highlanders, took off shoes, hose and gaiters, then undone our waist belts, pulled our kilts just far enough to cover our nakedness, tightened up our belts again to hold up our kilts, and then stepped in. As soon as we got to the other side all we had to do was dry our legs, dress them again and were in a few minutes ready for the road. But how did it fare with our Saxon friends wi' the breeks? Well, very badly indeed, especially if we were going through a sandy part of the country, their wet trousers taking up the sand, thus making it most difficult and painful to march.

During this long and trying march any man who fell out was deprived of his grog for that day, and, as every old soldier knows, this is a great punishment. No man was allowed to fall out for a drink of water, for when we came to water, every man drank as much as he wanted, then filled his water bottle; still there were thoughtless men among us who took no heed to the doctors on this, who were guided by the officers commanding on anything we drank and eat.

When about ten days' march from Kandahar, a young soldier of the 72nd Highlanders asked leave to fall out for a drink of water; if a man wants to fall out sick, he is accompanied to the rear by a non-commissioned officer, but, as already stated, no man can do so for a drink of water. It seemed to all accounts that this man neither filled his bottle or took a drink at the last place we had water. After asking the sergeant of his section several times to fall out for a drink, he rushed in among a lot of bushes and shot himself, where the rear guard found him some hours after.

The daily average of sleep we had was about three hours. General Roberts during the march had a guard composed of twenty-four picked men of the "Gordons," and the Highlanders who composed that guard were much inspired to hear their gallant general every night before going to sleep praying with the greatest sincerity to the Almighty for the safety of his army and the success of his mission.

It was sometimes 10 p.m. before we halted for the day but seldom later than 7 p.m. As soon as it was known where the army was to rest, one hundred men from each regiment, armed with picks and rifles marched to the nearest village for firewood and other provisions; a lieutenant in charge of each. As soon as we got to the village, the officer halted his men, and spoke to the people thus:—

> We are here not to make war wth you; we want wood, potatoes, etc., and will pay you a fair price for anything you are able to spare us. If you do not give us these things we will take them by force and pay you according to the destruction we make.

In every case that I have seen, the Afghans refused us with the utmost contempt. In these fatigue parties, as they were called, fifty men were armed with rifles and fifty men with picks and axes. The officer in command would order all the men armed to mount the walls and to keep a strict watch on the natives during the working of the men with picks and axes. The houses were ransacked at once, and anything in the shape of wood was pulled down and cut up in a way that it could be loaded on camels and mules which were ready at the gate to carry it to camp. As soon as the officer in command thought we had enough, he called on the chief or mayor of the village, made him look at what we had taken, and then paid him in silver whatever it was worth.

In many cases like this a whole village would be deprived of every piece of woodwork in it. But why should the army of General Roberts do things like this? Because two days after we left Ghiznee there was no wood of any kind to be had, the fuel used by the natives being cow and camel dung; and if we came to any place where straw, hay or such like could be had we could cook our food with it. So it was altogether a necessity for taking anything by force. And be it remembered that anything we took in such a way, the people were paid more than double its value.

The day we entered Ghiznee the 92nd Highlanders were the advance guard, and as we marched through the streets with our fine band of pipers playing the "Lads wi' the Kilts we noticed a very painful and curious sight. It was that of a white man mounted on a camel amongst a crowd of Afghans staring at us Highlanders as we passed along in grand array, with fixed bayonets. "The man is greeting us," said a voice from the ranks. And sure enough he was. "He is an Afghan with the leprosy; he is no European," said another. At any rate we were interested to know why he wept so bitterly at the sight of the kilted Highlanders. Our colonel at once gave the order to bring him to his presence and there explain who he was.

It was soon discovered that he was the son of a Private Dawson of the famous Black Watch, who was stolen from his parents by the Afghans some eighteen years before. All the English he could mutter was Johnny Dawson. He was a well-to-do camel driver, was circumcised, had five wives, and had all the nature and habits of the Afghan about him We took him to Kandahar, and shortly after found his father and mother in Australia; but when within a few miles from India he bolted back to Afghanistan and we never heard any more about him. At this same place we picked up a fine dog, which afterwards became a great hero in the regiment.

After distinguishing himself at several engagements he was named "Ghazee." He much resembled a West Highland collie, and woe to those who would come too close to the pipers, for he did not care a button for the band. As soon as the band started to play he would fall to the rear, pass the time among the rear companies till he heard the pipes start up again, then he would start away to the front like a shot, cock his lugs and tail and seemed to feel as proud as any of us. Much could be said of this curious dog, but as I have said his name was "Ghazee," which means warrior, he certainly did not make a fool of his name, and before concluding his brief history I must tell my readers that he had no less than nine wounds on his body, which brought him down to half his size. When we came home to Scotland after the war, Ghazee took very sick, and the officers put him into the veterinary hospital in Edinburgh, under no less a person than Professor Williams, who took several bullets out of his body. So much for Ghazee, of whom more *anon*.

As soon as we halted for the night and had our grog and other good things necessary to keep us alive and cheer our hearts for the trials we had, and those before us, we had three meals all in a lump, *viz.*, breakfast, dinner and supper, all these inside of one hour. Food for the animals sometimes could not be had at all, and even our own food was something awful, still we took it without a grumble, for we all well knew that it was the best we could get. During the march we halted two days to give the animals a rest, for they were dying in hundreds every day, not only for want of food, but from the long marches they had to undergo, and should it rain during the progress of a day's march, the tents, etc., on their backs would much increase in weight, so it is evident in such cases the poor brutes had to suffer.

It was sometimes 10 p.m. before we got our last meal, but it did not matter, we all had to be up at the first sound of the pibroch, at 12.30 a.m. The worst of all these were the hardships of outpost duty. For example: here is a corps on rear guard, coming in about three hours after the main body; some 200 men of these are told off for outpost duty, they are marched to their posts before they have a bite to eat or anything to drink, or a chance for a few minutes rest, and it may be some time before the orderly men can bring anything to them. I have seen cases where men in this march could not eat when their meals were brought to them, being so fatigued with hunger; but I feel proud to say that such cases were very rare among the ranks of the sons of dear old Scotia, *vide* General Robert's speech at the Mansion House, London, a few months afterwards.

Some days, although sixteen hours on the road, we did not go over fourteen miles, the nature of the country preventing us, and the number of animals falling dead with their loads. Other days we went rapidly along, covering as many as thirty miles. When going to rest we hardly ever took off our clothes; our kilts for a mattress, and a stone for a pillow. Such is only a very brief account of this piece of British pluck and endurance, and as Von Moltke said, "every man that went to Kandahar with General Roberts was a hero," it is here for my readers to judge.

On the 31st August we sighted Kandahar, And as the scouts of the 9th Lancers came rolling in, General Roberts ordered a halt. Every mounted officer of the staff was galloping here and there to ascertain where the best place would be to have a spy at the city and how our people were holding out. We had not halted ten minutes when a response was given to our signals. The first thing that was asked by our commander was, "Where is your Union Jack, General Primrose?" General Primrose at once replied that to have such a thing only drew the fire of the enemy on his quarters.

General Roberts at once gave the order to hoist the British flag and should it be shot down, replace it at once with another; this was about 7 a.m. on the 31st August, and as it was now a level plain for miles round, our army formed up in column of brigades with our fine regiments of cavalry feeling and clearing the way before us. As soon as the command was given to move forward, the Highlanders gave three terrible cheers which were at once taken up by the other regiments, so off we went in battle array to rescue our comrades, who were almost mad with pleasure at the glitter of our bayonets in the morning sunshine, as we advance to save them from the hands of such a cruel foe. We had not advanced five miles when Ayob Khan and his army of heroes of Maywand retired about two miles from the walls of Kandahar. Here they strongly entrenched themselves.

About 12 o'clock, noon, on the 31st August, the great march was completed, and as we piled arms outside the walls of Kandahar, many a soldier said: "I hope Ayob Khan will wait till the morrow, and give us a breath, so that we will be able to show him how to fight." He did wait. So now, on the morrow, one of the finest battles in the whole campaign takes place, and I shall try, in the best way I can, to describe how we won the day, and what the British can do when put fairly to the test.

CHAPTER 19

At Kandahar

After partaking of some coffee and bread, the order to advance was given, where to, we did not know; but as soon as we heard the firing of the 2nd Brigade we understood that it was for a reconnaissance, and sure enough this was what it was. General Roberts was anxious to feel his strength, and as soon as he did so, he ordered the whole army to retire and make Ayob Khan believe that we were beaten, Thus, as we retired, the whole of Ayob Khan's force was at our heels. As soon as we had a good look at them, the outposts were ordered to hold their ground, and were soon reinforced by the 1st and 3rd Brigades. After a few volleys the Afghans retired back into their trenches.

The only thing now that General Roberts and his army feared was that Ayob would bolt during the night. The object of our march from Cabul was not only to relieve the garrison, but to retake the two guns that Ayob Khan took from General Burrows on the 38th July, 1880, at Maywand, and also to rescue Lieutenant Hector McLean, of the R. H. Artillery, who was taken prisoner at Maywand. This gallant young officer, who belonged to Aberdeenshire, displayed some fine acts of heroism during that unfortunate battle, and when it became known to the Highlanders that a countryman of theirs was a prisoner in the hands of the enemy, our hearts beat with the wildest anxiety as to how we could rescue him.

About 11.30 a.m. the Highlanders and Gourkhas sent the flower of Ayob Khan's warriors flying before them. Lieutenant

McLean was at that time a prisoner in Ayob's tent. As soon as Ayob saw the pride of his army give way, he gave orders to his guard to shoot Lieutenant McLean, and then bolted with his train just in time to escape capture, for when our cavalry got to Helmund, Ayob Khan was not more than one mile ahead. Here is what the London *Punch* said of this gallant officer after the news of the battle reached London:—

Come gather around and I'll tell you a story,
Strange it may seem in martial days;
War is the theme and its issue is glory.
Silly old Troubadours jingled such lays,
What is the name of my hero? Write plain.
Soldier and Scotsman, it's Hector McLean.

Hector sounds well in a story of battle.
Homer had some .such old hero in Troy;
Schoolboys may doubt, but the roar and the rattle;
Cannon and smoke, that's the school of the boy.
Woolwich cadet, oh! so cruelly slain,
Why did they leave you, young Hector McLean.

Leave you, my lad, when your pals all around you,
Was there one comrade refused you his life?
War is full dear, but we could not afford you,
You, who rejoiced in the drum and the fife.
Ours is the loss, but to fame is the gain;
Why did they kill you, young Hector McLean?

Killed you, a prisoner left there and lonely,
Waiting in hope for the grasp of our hand;
Straining your ears for our cheering and only
Living to leap at the hilt of the brand.
Cursed be the murderers, children of Cain;
Those who betrayed you, brave Hector McLean!

How our hearts beat when we thought we could save you,
We were so near, yet you, boy, so far;
Unfurl the colours, we thought they would brave you,
Hope from the kilted lads to far Kandahar?

Strike up the pipes, and we'll at him again,
Roberts is marching to Hector McLean.

Merciless fate, when the Highlanders starte
Firm in the purpose to rescue a friend,
Out from the ambush the enemy started,
Came the last roll standard and that was the end.
Just as they breasted the hill from the plain,
Died like a soldier, young Hector MacLean.

Died! why, of course he met death like a hero,
Baring his breast while the enemy fled;
He was the victim, his jailor the Nero,
Pilling his body on heaps of the dead.
Still ere you fell, and were mixed with the slain,
Scotland was true to you. Hector MacLean.

After the reconnaissance of the 2nd Brigade, each brigade was told off to their respective posts, and we were in bed and fast asleep by 8 p.m. Reveille did not sound till about 7 a.m. next day which was a grand relief to us. By 9 a.m., General Roberts and his army were on the move; but long before this the Afghans were pelting shell and round shot at us, and had done considerable damage, nevertheless we heed them not. By 10 a.m. our forty pounders fired their first shot from Picket Hill. Just at this time General Roberts and staff came galloping up to the 92nd Highlanders, who were waiting for orders. As soon as our gallant general showed face the cheering from the Highlanders was terrible.

After the cheering, Major Geo. Stewart White, galloped to the front of the regiment and said, "92nd Highlanders, attention! The battalion will form for attack, No. 1 will extend from its left. No. 2 prolong the line to the left, etc., etc." So that in the inside of a few minutes we were off to meet the great warriors of Ayob Khan. It is now about 10.30 a.m. and the Battle of Kandahar is in full swing. The 92nd Highlanders are on the extreme right while their gallant countrymen, the 72nd, are next to them, and the Gourkhas. The advance is most rapid till we come to the first village, where the flower of the Afghan army is strongly entrenched. Here the fighting line is joined by the supports, and after taking a breath and firing a few shots, we advanced by half companies and sections by rushes. This we continued until within a hundred yards of them, but in the onslaught the "Gordons" lost heavily, and so did the gallant "Seventy-Twa."

Still we pressed forward with the greatest determination. The sound of the pibroch cheering us to the heart's core. The noise was so great, that the voice of any commander could not be heard; then along the supernumerary rank came the order, "As soon as the *bald head* of Major White is seen all will advance to the charge!" Major White in a few minutes was at the head of his gallant regiment, pulling off his helmet to show his bald head. At the signal we were off and at them, like tigers. in a few seconds we were in among them, and oh! what slaughter is now going on. Looking around me I see the wee Gourkhas, cutting right and left with their deadly knives; here again I feel myself parrying a blow, or making a lunge at some one—I do not know who. I am like the rest so full of excitement.

This dashing charge of the Highlanders made the rest of the battle easy, for we had swept away the pride of Ayob Khan's army. But it was in doing this that we suffered so severely. Among the "Gordons," Colour-Sergeant Fraser, fell, as also did Private Strachan, together with many others. In this dash the 72nd lost their colonel and Captain Frome, together with Sergeant Cameron, whom General Roberts mentioned as being a fine specimen of a Highland soldier. Sergeant Cameron, who was better known as "Curly Cameron," was a native of Deeside, and was a dear and affectionate friend of the writer.

After turning the tide of the day, we waited a few minutes to get a drink of water. Private MacLachlan, of my own company, when in the act of taking a drink of water, was attacked in the most daring manner by an Afghan who was lying down among the dead. He made straight for Mac's head; Mac parried off the sword with his left arm, and struck the Afghan right in the teeth with his left. Corporal MacPhail, I think it was, despatched the

Afghan with the bayonet. MacLachlan was, of course, badly cut on the forearm and top of his head. Many sights like this were seen during the battle, and the most lamentable of the whole was that of Captain Stratton, commanding the signalling corps under General Roberts. The battle was all over, and Captain Stratton, along with a lance-corporal of the 72nd, were going up Picket Hill to silence the forty pounders, when a wounded Afghan shot our gallant captain through the back, who fell dead at the corporal's feet. You may be sure the corporal put an end to this coward.

After partaking of a drink of water, we once more advanced to the attack. So on we went in the usual way, forcing everything before us by rushes, and in these encounters some fine acts of bravery were performed; particularly was this the case when we reached within 200 yards of the guns, which were pelting shell into us all day.

Major White's bald head still held good for the signal to charge. We are now about 100 yards from the guns. Major White rushes in front of the lines, off goes the helmet, and the glossy bald skin of our brave leader glitters in the sunshine. With one terrible bound the Highlanders are in among the gunners before they have time to reload, their infantry and cavalry having bolted at the first sound of the Highland war pipe. The gunners are cut down without mercy. A cheer goes up, and a shout, "The guns, the guns are ours!" Still we keep rushing on, leaving a few men to guard the guns we took. Away to our left are our own cavalry getting ready to make the dash on the now broken army of the once great Ayob Khan. Just as we turn the corner of the valley giving the Afghans chase, the whole of their camp appears in view and a wild rush was now made to rescue our countryman, Hector McLean.

At this time, be it remembered, we thought we had him safe, and it was in our wild search that the great tent of Ayob Khan fell into the hands of the 92nd Highlanders. The writer was among the first to find Lieutenant MacLean's body lying at the main entrance of Ayob's tent. When we found him he was quite warm, he was lying on his back, with a pleasant smile on his face. He was in his shirt sleeves with a book, with a green cover beside him; he had twelve bullets through his body. This is all I remember of the poor but brave Hector McLean, for his body was soon carried away by the band to headquarters hospital.

More than 2,000 tents fell into our hands, together with every gun they had. This fine piece of work, commencing with our march and ending with the battle, was the admiration of all Europe. It put an end to a most tedious and hard campaign which lasted from the 14th November, 1878, to the 1st September, 1880, and cost the Indian and home governments nineteen million pounds sterling.

In this battle of Kandahar the 92nd Highlanders had twenty killed and sixty-three wounded; the 72nd, seven killed and thirty-seven wounded. This was the European portion of the fighting line during the battle, for the other portion formed the reserve and was never called to the front, so they had none killed or wounded. The Pioneers and Gourkhas, however, who formed the other portion of the fighting line lost heavily also. Thus ended the Afghan war, where the 92nd Highlanders won two Victoria Crosses and nine distinguished conduct medals.

CHAPTER 20

Banquet at Meen Meer

On the morning of the 2nd of September the whole of our dead were buried, and the funeral was attended by General Roberts and his staff. All our dead, except Colonel Brownlow and Captain Frome, (both of the 72nd Highlanders) were rolled in blankets, and the two combined bands of the Highlanders led the way to the spot selected for the interment of our dead comrades. The dead march, which was "Scots wha hae," you may be sure, was played to perfection; nothing indeed in my estimation could surpass the solemnity of the sad picture, just think of it, readers! Here we are almost 10,000 soldiers who had marched 336 miles in twenty days under very trying circumstances and which has been admitted to be one of the greatest feats in military history, gathered together to pay the last respects to the bravest of the brave.

The finest leaders the British army ever knew are there; and it would be safe to say the flower of the British army also. Steadily along came the firing party, in full Highland garb, with our pipers on the reverse flank, making for their place in line. We are now at the head of the graves. The bodies are put into the graves here and there. The command is given "Fire three volleys in the air, with blank cartridge! Ready!" The volleys are fired. The pioneers are just getting ready to cover them up. The Presbyterian minister holds up his hands and in a moment the pioneers fall back into their places.

But why should this minister do this after the service? Because he knew almost every man that was put in their graves, and he wanted to say something about them. And so he did; and before he finished there was not one dry eye among us from General Roberts to the smallest drummer boy. The sight was sad in the extreme, and the writer will never forget it, nor will any man who was there.

But what about the Afghans who were laying in hundreds all over the field of battle, where the vultures and other beasts were tearing their bodies to pieces. Well, General Roberts gave orders to the garrison of Kandahar to have them buried, and a bad job they made of it, too. It took 600 men three days to do it, and in many cases the bodies were not more than one foot from the surface. The result of this was that cholera came to Kandahar, which played terrible havoc in the city and surrounding country not many weeks after.

After twenty-seven days rest in Kandahar, the Gordons started for India by way of the Bolan Pass. During our stay in Kandahar we pulled up to our old standard of strength and vigour; and the march down to India was a pleasure to us. After crossing the frontier we took train to Meen Meer, a very important station in the Punjab; here we were reviewed by Lord Ripon, then viceroy of India. The whole of General Robert's army was present, together with the Lahore and Meen Meer divisions, and many regiments too from different parts of India.

The review was a grand success especially the march past when the Highlanders and Gourkhas were going past the saluting point at the grand stand, where Lord Ripon stood, surrounded by all the glory of India, the cheering and throwing of flowers, etc., was, to say the least, enough to drive us Highlanders mad with joy and enthusiasm. Going past in column of double companies with seventy file per company, like a wall, brought forth the warmest admiration from our countrymen who had come from all parts of India to look at the heroes of Kandahar.

A day or so after the review Colonel Macdonald, editor of the *Civil and Military Gazette*, suggested in the columns of his fine paper, that the Scotchmen of the Punjab. should go shoulder to shoulder and do something to show their appreciation towards the Highlanders who had showered so many honours on their native land in the late campaign in Afghanistan.

The response to this hint was most wonderful, for in the inside of twenty-four hours, sixteen thousand *rupees* were thrown to the editor's door. Day after day money came pouring in, in the most liberal manner; a committee was soon formed which at once decided what should be done. All money received from those who were not Scotch was returned with thanks, so the whole affair was confined to the Scotchmen of the Punjab. Not many days after however, the two Highland Regiments *viz*: 72nd and 92nd Highlanders were invited to attend a banquet to be given in their honour at Meen Meer. The two regiments were ordered to parade early and by 11 a.m. all were there ready for action.

Tables were set for 1,200 men, but not inside any building, but in a most beautiful spot among trees. At noon the pipers sounded the fall in, and in a few minutes we were seated and enjoying ourselves to our hearts' content on the best things this world could give, and waited on, not by men, but by the highest ladies in the land, all dressed, if you please, in short dresses with different tartans, ready to give us anything that we called for. And how these ladies did laugh waiting on us wild "hieland sodgers," and such a happy time it was for us? After dinner Colonel Macdonald, of the *Civil and Military Gazette*, read an address to us. The officers of the two regiments replied and thanked our countrymen and ladies for such a glorious feast. We then took part in all kinds of games which are so dear to Scotsmen wherever they may be. The prizes for throwing the hammer and putting the shot, was over $100 for the first prize: the same was given for dancing and the singing of Gaelic songs. There were three lady judges in the Gaelic song competition and in this Private John McLeod of the 92nd Highlanders carried away the prize.

But in the Scotch singing competition the competitors were so numerous that the ladies could not decide who was who. No sooner was the stage empty than five or six men were ready to give a song. "Put doon my name, mom," "I can sing a fine Jacobite song" a voice would say. The ladies were bothered like this all day but they enjoyed the fun immensely. Nothing but Scotch songs could be accepted, so it is easy to understand the happy time we had, and every man who sung a song, no matter how short it was received ten *rupees* (five dollars) and there were over 400 men, who received that amount each. The closing point of the day was the tug-of-war between the Highlanders and Lowlanders, twenty-four men a-side. Mr. D. Ross of the Punjab and Delhi Railway, (an old school mate of the writer's) took command of the Highland team, and Major Scott of the 2nd Gourkhas took command of the lowland team, and after a very hard struggle the Highlanders won, this putting an end to one of the most happy days of my life.

To give the names of those present on this occasion would include the most prominent men in India, so in concluding this chapter it might suffice to say that the reception given by India to her soldiers will go to show how highly they appreciate anything which binds our great empire together, thus knowing full well that in a great measure depends greatly on the deeds and daring of her army in that great and wonderful country.

After a rest of nearly three months, the 92nd Highlanders are called again to arms, this time in South Africa, so on the 6th January 1881, we were on our way to Bombay, to embark for Durban, in the colony of Natal.

CHAPTER 21

South Africa

After a pleasant voyage we arrived at Durban on the 28th January, 1881. On landing the Rev. P. P. Martin, Presbyterian minister, read an address of welcome to us, and thousands crowded round us to shake hands. It rained all day and almost continually for three months after, for it was now the rainy season which makes camp life most miserable. After two hours' stay in Durban we took train for Petermaritzburg, the capital of Natal. Before leaving Durban the townspeople came with loads of pineapples to us and had a carload attached to our train.

We got a grand reception in Petermaritzburg, but did not wait for any time but at once proceeded with all haste to the front. We were joined here by the 75th Blue Jackets belonging to the warships in Durban. Those had several guns and one Gatling gun, which they were taking up to the seat of war at Lang's Neck. It seemed most comical to us Highlanders to see these "Tars" marching barefooted and carrying their shoes on their back but, that is the way Jack marches.

The march up to Mount Prospect where the headquarters of General Colley was, was not only miserable but most difficult. We could not have landed in a worse time, and from the day we started from Imburg our clothing and everything belonging to us was wringing wet, the roads were terrible, we never could go more than two miles an hour. So, after a hard struggle we reached General Colley's force on the 23rd February, 1881, and wondered very much when we got there to see things so quiet.

General Colley's force consisted at this time of the 30th Rifle Brigade, 58th Regiment, six guns and a few of the 3rd Dragoon Guards.

This small force had suffered three defeats before we joined them, and had lost many men. The majority of them wore bare-faced laddies as we Highlanders called them.

After arriving at Newcastle we were inspected by General Colley and his staff, and he was very much struck by our martial appearance. Nothing of any note took place till Saturday night On the 26th February, 1881, at about 8 p.m., a secret parade was ordered which consisted of about 554 men of all corps, viz.: 3rd Sixtieth 140 men, 58th Regiment 170, 92nd Highlanders 180, and 64 men of the Naval Brigade.

On the afternoon of the 25th February the writer was transferred from "H" to "F" Company, which was one of the most remarkable events in the Regiment. Why? Because "H" Company was one of the companies for the secret parade and not a sergeant of that company came back, and it is obvious that I would most certainly have been among the slain had I remained in "H" Company, but fate made it otherwise.

MAJABA (MAJUBA) HILL

Let me now pass over sad things and give you a picture of how matters are after that black Sunday morning's work. It was nearly 3 p.m. on the 27th February, 1881, before we had full details of the battle. It must be remembered, however, that the main body of General Colley's army were encamped at Mount Prospect which was fully live miles from the foot of Majaba.

The headquarters camp on learning the particulars were in the wildest excitement. Our General was killed! All his staff were taken prisoners, and the officers left in camp did not know what to do. The rank and file were anxious to go forward and reinforce our comrades who were retiring off the hill, but there was no leader! One officer seemed to be afraid of the other, and so before they came to any conclusion it was too dark to proceed to the rescue. Out of 180 men of the "Gordons" only eleven came back. On Monday, the 28th February, 1881, another great day of my life not to be forgotten, I was in charge of the burying party.

So under a flag of truce we proceeded up the steep slopes of Majaba for the purpose of claiming our dead and there bury them. When we got to the top of the hill there were hundreds of the Boers there waiting to see how and what we were going to do. We, the Highlanders, could easily identify our men by their dress, but as it rained all that night we could not tell their names until we undone their tunics, where we could see their regimental numbers. The rain made their bodies almost blue. We were soon to work however, and had them all buried before retreat. There was no funeral service there, each man was put in the grave as he fell in the most silent and solemn manner.

All this passes among us in silence, with the consoling hopes of revenge, but it stung the heart of every man in the gallant 92nd Highlanders, when in a week or so after that General Wood, V.C, etc. took command; and this is what that gallant soldier said after inspecting positions and the troops in his command. He telegraphed to the home government thus—"With the Highlanders, and two squadrons of the Hussars, and three guns of the R. H. Artillery, I will take Lang's Neck in two hours."

This message was sent about 4 p.m., and on the following day an answer was surely expected, and many an anxious one rushed to the headquarters the next day to hear the reply from home. We were in the middle of our dinner, when Mr. Cameron, of the London *Standard*, came riding past our camp and said the news was bad. Canteens, spoons, etc., were thrown in all directions, and all hands rushed in the wildest excitement for the headquarters tent, to hear particulars. We had not long to wait, for the reply to General Wood's message was posted on the flag staff, which was alongside of his tent. It read as follows:—"No more fighting; form an armistice."

The sight now is terrible. The curses on Gladstone; the hissing and howling is awful. Effigies are made of Mr Gladstone all over the Colony; carried shoulder high and burned in front of the Court House. Men got disgusted with the army, and many deserted, some, too, to the Boer Camp, and among the High-landers was one in particular who had over £20 in the Regimental Saving Bank, and was in possession of four good conduct badges; and over seventeen years service. That man threw all that away and deserted rather than stay.

This man was no other than Private Thomas Burns, "C" Company, 92nd Highlanders, and a native of Argyleshire. Desertions were a daily occurrence, until they formed a cordon of the Natal mounted police round camp. In short, every man from the general down felt stung in our national pride, which galled our military spirit, when it became known that we could not get a chance of wiping out the blotch which was now so painful to the heart's core.

After a stay of nine months' at Mount Prospect and New Castle, we marched down to Petermaritzburg, where the 92nd received a real Highland welcome. We were not one hour in camp when four barrels of beer, sixteen sheep and sixteen cases of Rob Roy whisky were carried to our camp by the people of that fine city. After six p.m. that night our camp was swarming with civilians from all parts of the country. Judging from what I see of Natal, I would say that about two-thirds of the white people are Scotch. After a few weeks rest in Petermaritzburg we take train for Durban, where we again receive another grand welcome. Here the regiments played *Rob Roy* for five nights, the writer taking part in it. We cleared £180 after paying all expenses. This money was given to the widows and wounded.

At last the most welcome news arrived. The 92nd Highlanders ordered home. What a happy thought! and that I have been spared to have passed all the dangers of such terrible sights and hardships, and that I will see my dear old mother once more and tell her about this battle and the other. Yes! these were the first things that ran through my mind at the first sound of ordered home.

CHAPTER 22

A View of Disaster

I cannot bid *adieu* to the colony of Natal without first giving a true and honest description of the Battle of Majaba, (Majuba). During operations the writer was asked by Major Nicholson, (late Bengal Staff Corps) editor of the *Times*, of Natal, to send a weekly letter of the doings of the army at the front. From week to week my letters appeared in that paper, and other papers in the colony copied them; so that I am in possession of the most accurate accounts of that sad campaign.

The outstanding feature of this campaign in the Transvaal in 1881 was the unfortunate disaster to British arms on Majaba Hill. It was an event which stung our national pride. After the first stun of defeat had left the vision dear, it was easy to understand that a blunder had been committed, but it was not so easy to say by whom. The officer on whom had rested the responsibility of the movement was dead; and men hesitate to speak freely of the shortcomings of those who are no longer able to defend themselves, who have, indeed, paid with their life for the frailty of their judgement. In most accounts—official and otherwise—of the disaster, credit is given to the British officers and men for doing their best to uphold the honour of British arms, but in one this credit is taken away and the British troops are charged with getting into what is not very euphemistically termed "a funk," and with bolting in face of the enemy.

These charges, among others, are to be found in a passage interpolated In the *Cruise of the Bacchante*, by Canon Dalton, who acted as editor for the *Young Prince of Wales*, and he gives the following narrative of the disaster which certainly cannot be supported by known facts.

> A funk became established among our men. The order to fix bayonets and charge down upon the advancing Boers was not executed. Weary and panic-stricken the English turned and fled. Sir Geo. Colley, at the first rush, was shot through the head. With a loud cry of fright and despair the English flung themselves over the edge of Majaba; the Boers poured on, and fired on them below as they ran like game. The Boers had one man killed and five men wounded; the English, ninety-two killed and 134 wounded and fifty-nine prisoners. There have been cases when a defeat, invited by a mistake of a British general, has been saved by the courage of the men, but it was not so at Majaba. The men made no effort to turn the fortune of the day. They commenced to run before the Boers reached the top of the hill. The reserves bolted almost before they bad fired a shot.—Vol. 1., page 369.

Such a statement as that in the *Cruise of the Bacchante* might have been treated with dignified silence, or it might have been met with a direct denial. But, probably a better way than either is to tell simply and plainly the true story of Majaba. It has never been fairly told. Gross misrepresentations have prevailed, alike with regard to the action and the causes which led to defeat. The circumstances of the moment were not favourable for the chronicling of events. The newspaper correspondents present were caught up in the whirl of disaster and could do little more than note the outstanding points at the time of the crisis. Those whose duty it was to furnish official details could tell all that was desired in a few pregnant sentences. But the memory of the defeat has seated itself deeply in the minds of many of those who survived the engagement, and the desire that their honour and the honour of their corps should be vindicated has induced the officers of the 92nd Highlanders to furnish the statements from which the details of these articles are drawn.

Although not a third of the whole fighting force the 92nd were more strongly represented than any of the other corps engaged, and their disposition was such that the narrative from their various points of view practically covers the whole ground. The documents from which the facts are partly taken have been obtained from all the officers present, by Lieutenant-Colonel McBean, who served for thirty years under the flag of the "Gay Gordons," and who had some few years before the Majaba disaster, retired with the rank of Lieutenant-Colonel Commanding.

Feeling aggrieved at the obloquy attempted to be cast on his gallant regiment, he has placed the document at the disposal of the writer, so that the readers of the *Scottish Canadian*, in the first instance, might have the truth about the Battle of Majaba. On the 20th December, 1880, the Boers, repudiating the annexation of the Transvaal territory to the British Crown, threw down the gage of battle. The Boers, or Dutch colonists, were hardy men, admirable rifle shots, and possessed a quiet resolute courage which gave them great advantage in the form of warfare in which they were engaged. In the Transvaal at the time hostilities opened there were not sufficient British troops to quell the Boer rising, and reinforcements were sent forward from the Cape with all possible speed.

Among the reinforcements were the 92nd Gordon Highlanders who reached Sir George Pomeroy Colley's Camp, on Wednesday, the 23rd February, 1881. The regiment numbered 629 of all ranks, and was under the command of Lieutenant-Colonel G. H. Parker. General Colley at Lang's Neck suffered severely at the hands of the enemy, but with this new instrument of war in his hand a fair means was afforded of vindicating the supremacy of British arms. The 92nd Highlanders was no collection of raw recruits, but a body of bronzed and war-stained veterans. They had fought at Charasia and Cabul with General Roberts, with a cool courage, which called forth the warmest praise from their victorious chief.

Under Roberts, they had also performed the famous march

to crush Ayoob Khan at Kandahar, during its progress obtaining distinction for their superior powers of endurance, their fine physique, wide chest measurement, and splendid muscular development It was this body of men who joined General Colley at Mount Prospect, prepared to a man to match their strength, courage, and skill against the Boer marksmen.

Three nights after we joined the camp, on Saturday, 26th February, the order for action came. General Colley had resolved upon his course; what that course was he for the time kept to himself. Not a soul beyond the staff knew that any movement was impending, and young as the night was, one officer at least had turned in to bed. At eight o'clock orders were issued for troops to parade an hour and a half later with 70 rounds of ammunition, three days rations, great coats and blankets. The following were the troops called out: Two companies 3rd 60th Rifles, under command of Captain Smith; two companies 58th Regiment, under Captain Morris, three companies of 92nd Highlanders, under Major Hay, and 64 men of the Naval Brigade, under the charge of Commander Romilly, a total force of 554 men.

The troops mustered at headuarters camp at 10 o'clock, marched off in silence, not a soul in the ranks as yet knowing anything of their destination. General Sir George Colley, commanded in person. As the men tramped along, however, making as little noise as possible, dark as the night was light enough obtained to see in front towering up against the sky, about four miles distant the flat topped mountain of Majaba, and it began to be understood, that that was the end and aim of the night march. The men were heavily laden with their rations ammunition and other impediments, and when shortly after starting they left the level and began a winding climb up the side of the Umguala Mountain, the march became extremely tiresome.

At this point about eleven o'clock two companies of the 60th Rifles and one of the 92nd were detached to keep communication with the camp and thus leaving 200 men behind, the remaining 350 marched along a hill path on the right towards

Majaba. At the base of this great mountain, which rises 6,500 feet above sea level, the serious work of the march began. The sides of the mountain are rugged and precipitous, with great boulders here and there and at many points the men had to toil up the steep ascent hand-over-hand. Writing the day after when he accompanied a party of men up to bury the dead, Captain Forbes McBean, Colonel McBean's son says:

It was a fearful climb and it is a perfect mystery to me, how men with pouches full of ammunition, carrying rolled blankets and great coats and three days rations, could ever have got up in daylight much less on a pitch dark night.

About one o'clock a company of the 92nd got lost on the hillside and the other company had to wait a whole hour, until the staff, which went in search of the strayed men were able to bring them back. The loading files of the 58th were the first to reach the top, this was about four o'clock in the morning, and the last of the 92nd got up about half-past five. When daylight permitted the position to be reconnoitred it was found to be a plateau bounded by a steep brow, to quote the regimental records which were written by Colonel—later Major-General—G. S. White, V.C, K.C.B., lately commanding the 92nd Highlanders. The position held against the enemy was a mile circumference. From the centre and crest of this plateau the ground sloped downwards towards the brow, so that the plateau was exposed to a fire from the lower ground all round, but was especially searched out from a ridge not included in the position, but which was within easy rifle range of its north-west angle.

The approaches to the brow below were nearly all concealed from the view of the defenders on the top. The slope of the hill leading up to the brow, is broken by natural terraces, which run nearly round the hill, and which afforded the enemy, under cover of his firing parties placed for the purpose, opportunity of collecting in force on any point, and to circuit round the hill, without coming under the fire or observation of the defenders. In addition, it must be added that the Boer camp, to command which was the only possible reason for the movement, was beyond rifle range of the position, and General Colley had neglected or perhaps been unable to take with him mountain guns, which might, says Major, the Hon. J, S. Napier, who saw the action in progress, have been used from Majaba Heights with good effect as a covering fire to an infantry attack on the Boer camp from below.

It must also be stated that there was no water to be found on the summit. A circuit of about a mile had to be manned by 350 men, which was not homogeneous, but composed of detachments from three different corps, and the members of which were exhausted by their harassing night march. The necessity for extending the men so much was due to the impossibility of observing an enemy's approach, or determining at what point his attack might be delivered. The defence was distributed as follows:—

The Highlanders being placed by Major Macgregor, who was on the general's staff, to the 92nd were given the western brow and part of the northern. One company was extended and the other formed a support, not a reserve. Behind the rocky ridge in the centre of the plateau, the 58th held the eastern and part of the northern brow, their second company being in support, along with the company of the 92nd. The sailors held the southern corner of the plateau: sixteen men were posted at eleven, and a few at five. Lieutenant Hector Macdonald held a knoll on the south face with eighteen men, and Lieutenants Wright and Hamilton were in command of the second line of Highlanders who held the western brow.

CHAPTER 23

Eyewitness to Catastrophe

Instead of ordering the men to form such entrenchments as might have been possible in the time at his disposal before daylight, and before any Boer attack could be made upon him, General Colley ordered them to rest in their positions. He walked round the posts, saying to the troops: "All I ask you is to hold this hill three days." Later on, when the hill was swept with the enemy's fire, and where no working party could live, he thought of entrenching, and, accompanied by Commander Romilly, went in search of a site, but it was too late then, and poor Romilly was shot dead by the general's side. The precious time had been wasted, and an unsheltered handful of men had to meet the concentrated fire of 2,000 marksmen, firing from perfect cover, and from every point of vantage.

Shortly after 6 a.m., when just light, (says Captain Wright), in his statement, a patrol of Boers went round the base of the hill unsuspectingly, when a shot was fired from the 3rd 60th against orders, which were not to bring on an engagement if it could be avoided. However, that shot told a tale, and the Boers galloped back to their camps with it immediately. All the camps were like wasps' nests disturbed, and it really was an imposing sight to see that Sunday morning all turn out, fires lighted for breakfast, and then a morning hymn sung, after which all the waggons were inspanned, and the Boers turned out for battle. A storming party of about 200 men immediately rode under the second ridge. By crossing round under the naval brigade's position they could do it without being seen. There they left their horses (all the Boer army were mounted), and climbed right under the hill, where we could not see them without going to the very edge of the hill and exposing ourselves entirely to the fire from the two ridges. In this position we remained till about noon, the Boers climbing towards us step by step, and I may almost say unsuspected by any but Hamilton and myself.

Twice I went to the general and told him we couldn't hold our position with so few men (about seven to one), if any serious attack were made. All he said was: "Hold the place three days." General Schmidt, who commanded the Boers' attacking party that day, told Major Douglas and Captain Dick Cunyngham, of the 92nd, that he had 2,000 rifles employed in the attack. It thus became a question of time when the Boers would concentrate the fire of their covering parties, and deliver their attack on some point in the line which occupied the brow. Once in possession of the brow they had but to lie down in the cover which it afforded, and search out the interior with their fire. At about 12.30 o'clock the enemy having quietly completed all his preparations fired a very heavy volley direct on the few men who were occupying the brow immediately opposite the ridge (on the western face), putting half of them *hors de combat* (out of action).

By this time the support had been greatly decreased by the call for reinforcements from different points, to keep down the fire and approach of the Boers, whose parties now nearly surrounded the hill. The few men left in support, chiefly sailors and 58th men, were now brought up towards the western face, but were halted short of the position from which our men had been driven. Finding that they could not shoot over the brow they were withdrawn, and formed behind the ridge in centre of plateau. The Boers then, led by a few *Kaffirs*, pushed in great force into the gap thus left in the western face, and there established took the north face in flank and reverse, and rendered it untenable. Almost immediately after the Boers showed in force on the northeast angle on a *koppie*, which is the highest point on Majaba top.

Our men now formed behind the central ridge, fixed bayonets, and as the unequal fire contest could not be long doubtful, Lieutenant Hamilton suggested to Sir Geo. Colley, that the men should he ordered to charge. Sir George replied: "Not yet; wait till they cross the open, and then we will give them a volley and charge." But the Boers were not likely to give up the advantages of their better positions, and the superiority of their many rifles, to cross the open and risk shock tactics with an enemy trained to close order fighting, and our men taken in front from the west, in flank, and rear, from the knoll and from the hollow, fell rapidly. By this time our ammunition was getting low, and the pouches of the men were being replenished from those of our dead comrades.

At last the line broke, but not before General Colley said: "Retire, men, the best way you can, for the ground is too steep for an orderly retreat!" Before the last position was yielded, the number was reduced to 60 or 70 men, and there was a line of killed and wounded, chiefly 92nd, to mark the ground. About 1 p.m. we saw some heads appearing over the top. The 92nd rushed forward in a body and drove them for the moment back. We lost about 50 killed and wounded. Then, strange to say, the word to cease fire came distinctly to where Hay and I were, and immediately after retire. We all ran back to the ridge in the middle of the hill, which allowed the Boers to gain the hill. Then came the murder!

In the meantime more Boers came up round where the sailors were, and began to fire into the hospital, and so took us in rear. Hamilton and I both went to the general, and asked to be allowed to charge. "Wait," he said, "send a volley or two first; I will give the order."

Hamilton then said to me. "Let us call on the Highlanders, and charge on our own account; are you ready, Harry!" I answered yes; drew my claymore and laid it beside me. I had no sooner done so, when Hamilton fell wounded at my side. Macgregor came up then and said, "We've got to die now."

Just then I heard the general say, "Retire in as orderly a manner as you can," when they all jumped up and ran to the rear. Hay and I and two men of ours remained where we were, all using rifles and firing our best; Macdonald still held his position and would not budge, neither would we. About a quarter of an hour after the retirement no firing had been going on from the rest of our troops, which neither Hay nor I could understand; as we thought by retiring it was meant to hold the brow on the east side where the 58th were posted. We were now being sorely pressed, hiding our bodies behind stones, and for another five minutes the unequal combat went on. Then Hay said, "The battle's over, we can't fight a multitude; let us try and get away."

So off we four started in the direction which the others had previously taken, under a most awful volley from the Boers on the Navy side, and the ridge where we had been latterly firing at the enemy only twenty yards distant. Both the men were killed. Hay was shot on the leg and arm, and I was hit on the foot and turned head over heels. I had to crawl on my stomach, a yard or two back to get my rifle and so lost Hay, who got under cover somewhere.

I will now close Lieutenant Wright's statement and leave the account to another stage.

Meantime, let me turn to the narrative of Major (later Major General) Hay, who was in command of the two companies of the 92nd. He says the objectionable sentences in the *Bacchante* account of the battle, which he declares to be erroneous from beginning to end, and he refutes them on one point. He points out that what is called in official documents a reserve, was no reserve, but merely a support, which although originally consisting of three companies, had sent forward so many reinforcements to the fighting line; that when the final attack was made there were only twenty-four men left. He describes as rubbish the *Bacchante* statement that the order to fix bayonets and charge down on the advancing Boers was not executed. Bayonets, he says, were fixed, but he supports the records and Lieutenant Wright in declaring that no order was given to charge. Hamilton he says asked Sir G. Colley to allow the men to charge, but Sir George refused to do so, and in his opinion was right in refusing.

> There was nothing to charge. There was not a Boer to be seen. From the position we then occupied the ground went down in a gentle slope for a short distance and then came a steep descent. The Boers had collected just where the steep descent began and without being seen themselves their fire swept the glacis-like slope which would have had to be crossed before they could be reached, and besides the slopes were under a heavy fire from a ridge only four hundred yards off. A charge under such circumstances would in my opinion have been madness and could have done no good at any rate.

Without entering into the merits of this point of tactics we emphasise the conclusion that the request of these officers to be allowed to charge and the willingness of the men to follow, show how eager they were to grapple at close quarters with the foe.

> The line, (he continues), remained firing in the direction of the Boers till it received the order to retire. He (General Colley) I suppose considered there was nothing to be gained by holding on any longer, firing at an invisible enemy. His men were being shot down without being able to inflict any loss upon the enemy. It was a mere matter of time how long the unequal contest could last—simply depended on how long it would take to finish off the

survivors.

As soon as the ridge was left, and not till then the Boers came on firing as fast as they could. There was nothing the men could do. They stood until they were ordered to retire. There were no reserves and the supports did not bolt. We did certainly go before the Boers reached us, for the simple reason that the Boers did not leave their cover till we had retired. I have met people who thought that the Boers had charged and driven us off the hill. Had they done so the tale would be quite different to relate. It was the crushing fire that compelled us to retire, and until we had retired not a Boer was to be seen.

General Colley, continues Major, seeing the small number of men remaining and these few were being mowed down without in any way being able to silence the enemy's fire, gave the order for them to retire as best they could. This they did on the eastern slope of the plateau but part of the 58th, who held that position, and who had also had their ranks terribly thinned, were unable any longer to hold it. So it was with the few men left there, as well as those who had retired, from what I may call the second position behind the low central ridge. The men under Lieutenant Hector Macdonald on the hillock, (with the exception of one or two only being either killed or wounded) were there surrounded and either killed or shot down.

It is imagined by many that the Boers actually gained the plateau and drove the defenders off it, sending them back from each position. The Boers never showed themselves at all if they could help it, and never to such an extent as to allow a single effective volley to be delivered at them. The defenders lost each position from the few remaining men left to hold it, being the whole time under a well directed fire, which they were unable to return with any effect. It was like men in the open exposed to the fire of an entrenched enemy; it was only a matter of time when they had so shot down the men in the open that they could leave their entrenchments without any chance of opposition.

Out of eight officers of the 92nd Highlanders, only one came back, Captain Singleton, died of his wounds, all the others were wounded or taken prisoners; Colour-Sergeant Fraser was buried with the company's pay which he had under his kilt. But why? because we were under a flag of truce and could not take anything from the dead, for the Boers were there watching; Sergeant Tulloch, the only sergeant of the 92nd who escaped, had ten pounds sent to him by a gentleman in Natal, three years after the battle, for a piece of heroism that was never recorded, and the sergeant was too proud to let any person know about it. The gentleman, it appears, was travelling through the Transvaal and one night fell in with a lot of Boers who were talking about the Majaba, and three of them were relating a story, when trying to take prisoner one of the Highlanders.

In short, Sergeant Tulloch was asked to hand over his rifle, instead of doing so, he broke it against a stone, then drew his sword and cut and wounded three or four of them, then leaped over the precipice landing on a tree some 30 feet below; here the sergeant remained all night; and at daybreak got into camp. Sergeant Tulloch, who is a powerful Highlander from Culloden, was badly hurt on the back after the jump, so much so, that he could not bear the knapsack, so the colonel made him provost-sergeant.

General Colley was the only person of all the killed that got a coffin; all the others were buried just as they fell. During the night the Boers stripped the dead of all watches, rings, etc. Lieutenant Macdonald, who was among the prisoners had the painful duty of handing over his claymore, which he got from the officers of the regiment a few months before as a present, but it was returned to him after the settlement of the Commission.

At the time of the battle. General Colley had under his command more than 2,000 men, and yet, when it was known that our men were retiring, nothing could be done. Why? Because the general and his staff were in the wrong place. Whoever heard of a general leaving the main body and going out with a reconnaissance, a force that is not supposed to fight at all. This was the great wonder of all who went up the Majaba, and those in camp. There is a splendid monument on the top of Majaba for those of the 92nd who fell.

After Majaba about 900 men deserted, the majority going from the 94th Regiment or 2nd Connaught Rangers. There were several Irishmen fighting against us, one of them a doctor, who Mr. Cameron of the *Standard* called a renegade, in front of the whole Boer army. Cameron at this time was a prisoner, but was soon after released by General Joubert. The doctor's name was an assumed one and I forget it.

CHAPTER 24

Return to Scotland

The Boers are a very conservative race of people; they hate railways or anything their fathers did not use, and of course are a great hindrance to the British colonists. A few of us Highlanders were invited one day (after the war, of course) to drink some gin with them and have a good time; on entering the farmyard the first thing we noticed was the old-fashioned gate which took two of us to open. "Say, Boss, why don't you fix that gate of yours? Why, it takes no less than two men to open it."

"Oh," replied our host, "mine fadder done with it, so can I."

They are not kind to strangers; they are sulky and stiff. Among the intelligent class, however, (and they are very few) they are fond of British people. There are no poor among them; they all help each other; they do not care for money; they bring grain, wool and other things to market and get all supplies in exchange. All money used among them is English. The greatest ambition of a Boer is to have a fine horse and a good rifle. Should you meet one on the road and ask him how many miles it is to such a place, he takes a good look at your horse first, then at you; he will then say about five hours' ride as the case might be. There are no milestones in that country; but they are splendid judges of man and beast travelling.

During the armistice at Mount Prospect, Lady Florence Dixie, who was war correspondent to the *London Daily News*, sent a challenge to the Boer camp, to shoot at 200 yards, any of their force. The challenge was taken up, and arrangements made, bottles were hung up on a tree, which were the best things to be had at the time. Out of the first twenty the Boers brought down nine, but Lady Florence brought down no less than fifteen. Lady Florence was dressed so that the Boer thought it was a man he was firing against; and it can easily be imagined how small he felt, when the best shot in all the Transvaal was beaten by a Scotch lady. All the world knows the shooting propensities of this fine lady, and it was only the other day I read in the papers that she is now pining over the many beautiful stags and other game she killed in her hunting tours all over the world.

When stationed at New Castle, a small town near Mount Prospect, a lot of Highlanders and blue jackets were down town for a day's fun. By this time everything was all settled, and we were commencing to forget the days gone by. I must state first that Highlanders and blue jackets were very thick, and it was seldom you could see a tar going to town without some of the "Jocks" with them—Jocks was what the sailors called us Highlanders, and we, in return, called them Jacks. It was on an afternoon sometime in September, I think, a lot of us had two and three days' pass. After getting into town, and making some purchases, a lot of us made for the Phoenix Hotel, where we intended to put up.

As soon as we entered a rush was made for the billiard table, where we played several games. About 7 p.m. Boers and all kinds of people crowded in, and seemed to enjoy looking at the Highlanders in their bare legs playing with the sailors. The best of goodwill prevailed all round, for none of the sailors or Highlanders would call a round except all joined in. About 10 p.m. the Scotch whiskey was commencing to show itself, and of course the Boers could not hold their tongue about Majaba, for their eyes were red with the gin. Their boasting continued, notwithstanding the appeals of Mr. Munro, the manager of the hotel.

At last Sergeant John Macfadyen, of the Highlanders, stood up on a chair and swore if there were any more such talk he and his comrades would clear the house. This was received with groans. Before the sound of the groans ceased the sailors were in among them, with the "bare 'ands" hitting hard, right and left, and the Highlanders with their belts. The numbers were about equal, and the fight was, to say the least, fought with a vengeance by us. At the first go off we cleared the house in fifteen minutes, but they commenced to gather again. Meantime our men came crowding down, all the doors were soon closed, and we continued our fun, but there was not a whole chair in the place.

About an hour or so after the scuffle they (the Boers), commenced to break the windows, and crying for us to come out. After making arrangements about how we should give them a hiding, the back door was opened, when we all rushed out, and before you could say "Jack Robinson" the Highlanders and sailors were at them again. Jack hitting right and left, and his brother Jock with his belt knocking them into fits. The battle continued about twenty minutes, and never a crowd of men got such a flogging as did these Dutchmen.

That night the writer was cut badly on the face, and the mark always reminds him of the boys in the red and blue. Nearly every man of us had a mark of some kind, while almost all our Boer friends had to be carried home, and four died over the affair, so that we did not leave the country altogether without being avenged for our many dead comrades which we left behind us.

Yes, we are now homeward bound, and what is sweeter to a soldier who has fought through shot and shell, than the news of peace and home? I am now fourteen years absent from home. I have told you many things I have seen and done, but nothing inspires my Highland blood greater than the thought of home, and that I shall see my native hills again, where in my boyhood my happy days were spent. Oh! such happy memories go flowing through my brain, all at the thought of home.

I have often wondered how it was that I loved Scotland so much which gave me and mine so little, for my father was a poor man and his fathers before him, and yet the very name of Scotland has a charm on me. I have heard it said that a Scotsman does not show any love to Scotland till he leaves it, and from my own experience I believe this to be true. At any rate I am proud of the race, and can well testify to their deeds and daring in the field of battle. Their devotion to do their duty faithfully and well is one of their most conspicuous characteristics.

So much for my countrymen as soldiers; and before I conclude this chapter I must say a word about the pipers in front of an enemy. The bagpipes is the only music used now in the field of battle They play you into the field, and out of it. They stick with the fighting line during the struggle, and blow up whenever they see the bayonets going on the rifles. They work independently, each piper or pipers to his own company, but they must be good pipers who can even double and play the charge say fifty yards.

In Afghanistan our pipers took some time before they could do this, but they soon came to be able to do it to perfection. Outsiders may say as they like but I believe that the courage of the Highlanders would often fail if it were not for the strain of the pibroch. But where is the band on active service? All the band instruments are in large boxes in charge of the quarter guard: and the acting bandsmen in the ranks, and the full bandsmen are with the ambulance in rear. On the way to the seat of war they are taught by the regimental doctors how to attend wounded men and how to apply bandages, etc. etc. In a Highland regiment the bugle is seldom used in action. The drummers are generally helping the pioneers serving out ammunition to the fighting line which is the most dangerous post in the field. The artillery is always pretty safe in a general engagement—as an example there were not six artillery men killed in the whole Afghan war.

So now in concluding the story of my life abroad let me fall back for a while and tall you something of the Clach boys that mustered with me fourteen years before at the head of Tomnahurich Street. Oh, how sad it is to relate, and as I am about to pen it my heart seems to burst with grief, but I must tell it. Out of the twelve I am the only one living! When I think of it even to this day I feel strange. To be brief, two died in India, three of them are lying far away in Kandahar, and the other six are asleep on the top of the wild Majaba. When on furlough in Inverness I visited all their mothers and told them how their boys fell with their faces to the foe.

Private John MacRae's mother, who lived in King Street Inverness, when she saw me coming up the stair, fainted at the very sight of the red coat. Poor John was a fine looking soldier and he was one of the twelve. At Majaba he was mortally wounded and I buried him beside his cousin Colin MacRae.

On the 18th December, 1881, the 92nd Highlanders embarked for Old England on board the transport ship *Calabria*. Nothing of any note took place till we were crossing the line; and that was on New Year's day, 1882. We had a splendid dinner of course on that day, and an extra pint of porter given each man.

The *Calabria* was not a navy boat, consequently we soldiers had more liberty. We had about ten days bad weather, and down below could be heard the chorus among us—

Rolling home to bonnie Scotland,
Rolling home dear land to thee,
Rolling home to dear auld Scotland,
Rolling home across the sea.

On the 29th January, about six a.m., the lookout on the masthead shouted, "Land on the starboard bow." As everything was then still, every man awake heard the cry, all came rushing up out of our hammocks, and as soon as we saw the shores of Old England the cheering knew no bounds. Shortly after passing through the Needles, several steamboats came alongside, among them on board were the Duke of Cambridge, and many others from Pall Mall. Sailing into Portsmouth along the whole way there were thousands of people cheering us, and when passing the Soldier's Home in Queen Street, we were nearly suffocated with flowers, and after a hard struggle through the crowd, we arrived in comfortable barracks.

After getting somewhat settled down in barracks, the fur-

103

loughs commenced, and with the first batch I took the opportunity. So under command of an officer we were marched to the
station, 240 men in all; all, too, bound for Scotland. After a few
hours' run we arrived in the big town of London; here we had
to wait some time for the Scotch express. While waiting on the
train, the station was swarming with people who came to look,
and of course have a talk with us.

We were soon on our way to the land o'cakes, and many of
us were over the border before we knew it. My ticket was for
Inverness, and I changed at Glasgow. On my way north, seeing
the Highland heather for the first time, I suggested to jump
out the first chance and nave a sprig in my bonnet, but when I
looked round the train was gone: this was at a place called Nairn,
about sixteen miles from Inverness. The next train would not be
for some hours, so arming myself with some provisions, I took
to the road which I knew well. It was just two o'clock when I
found myself walking up Petty Street.

I was expecting every minute that someone would know me,
but no; and I was the same; I was trying to see some that I knew,
but I could see none. I felt disappointed; but as I turned down
Ingle Street, met my brother, where after a shake of the hand,
we drove home. When my old mother saw me she made a rush
at me, and taking me in her powerful arms she nearly kissed the
cheek off me. The house was soon crowded, and my mother was
jumping with joy at the return of her soldier son. A few days
after my arrival in my native town I received an invitation to attend a dinner in the Caledonian Hotel. Here I was toasted in all
shapes, and at the end received a purse and twenty-five pounds.
After putting in six weeks of the most enjoyable days I ever had,
I took train to Glasgow to visit a sister and brother.

On leaving Inverness, there was quite a crowd to see me
away, and my hand was sore for sometime by the snaking of
hands. After a few days' stay in Glasgow I returned to the regiment, which was stationed at Portsmouth; here we remained till
October, 1882. We then went to Edinburgh, "Scotia's darling
city," leaving Portsmouth on 6th October. On landing at Grant-

on pier, thousands of people came to meet us. After forming up, the colonel taking off his bonnet shouted three cheers for auld Scotland; you may be sure we cheered. Yes, it was a cheer that I or anyone in the ranks that day will not forget. Our colonel then gave the command, "Highlanders, attention! Fours right; to Auld Reekie, quick march!" The band then struck up, "Within a Mile o' Edinbro Toon."

We received a grand reception, and soon won the respect of the people. After a few months soldiering in Edinburgh my wound broke out, owing to a fall, and I was obliged to go to hospital. After passing a board of doctors I was invalided, and discharged on March 24th, 1884, with a pension for life. This after serving my Queen and country for seventeen years and 129 days in the famous "Gordon Highlanders." It was like leaving home parting with so many old comrades, and as the band of pipers played me out, I felt terribly sad. In conclusion, I must add that now my story is finished, I have told it in a simple and true way, which has been my aim from beginning to end.

For freen's that I lo'ed they are scattered far and wide,
And dim, dim's the past's misty track,
And some are dead and gone, oh, my tears they winna hide,
For it's sad, oh, it's sad lookin' back.

LEONAUR

ALSO FROM LEONAUR

AVAILABLE IN SOFTCOVER OR HARDCOVER WITH DUST JACKET

THE RELUCTANT REBEL *by William G. Stevenson*—A young Kentuckian's experiences in the Confederate Infantry & Cavalry during the American Civil War..

BOOTS AND SADDLES *by Elizabeth B. Custer*—The experiences of General Custer's Wife on the Western Plains.

FANNIE BEERS' CIVIL WAR *by Fannie A. Beers*—A Confederate Lady's Experiences of Nursing During the Campaigns & Battles of the American Civil War.

LADY SALE'S AFGHANISTAN *by Florentia Sale*—An Indomitable Victorian Lady's Account of the Retreat from Kabul During the First Afghan War.

THE TWO WARS OF MRS DUBERLY *by Frances Isabella Duberly*—An Intrepid Victorian Lady's Experience of the Crimea and Indian Mutiny.

THE REBELLIOUS DUCHESS *by Paul F. S. Dermoncourt*—The Adventures of the Duchess of Berri and Her Attempt to Overthrow French Monarchy.

LADIES OF WATERLOO *by Charlotte A. Eaton, Magdalene de Lancey & Juana Smith*—The Experiences of Three Women During the Campaign of 1815: Waterloo Days by Charlotte A. Eaton, A Week at Waterloo by Magdalene de Lancey & Juana's Story by Juana Smith.

TWO YEARS BEFORE THE MAST *by Richard Henry Dana. Jr.*—The account of one young man's experiences serving on board a sailing brig—the Penelope—bound for California, between the years 1834-36.

A SAILOR OF KING GEORGE *by Frederick Hoffman*—From Midshipman to Captain—Recollections of War at Sea in the Napoleonic Age 1793-1815.

LORDS OF THE SEA *by A. T. Mahan*—Great Captains of the Royal Navy During the Age of Sail.

COGGESHALL'S VOYAGES: VOLUME 1 *by George Coggeshall*—The Recollections of an American Schooner Captain.

COGGESHALL'S VOYAGES: VOLUME 2 *by George Coggeshall*—The Recollections of an American Schooner Captain.

TWILIGHT OF EMPIRE *by Sir Thomas Ussher & Sir George Cockburn*—Two accounts of Napoleon's Journeys in Exile to Elba and St. Helena: Narrative of Events by Sir Thomas Ussher & Napoleon's Last Voyage: Extract of a diary by Sir George Cockburn.

AVAILABLE ONLINE AT www.leonaur.com
AND FROM ALL GOOD BOOK STORES
07/09

LEONAUR

ALSO FROM LEONAUR

AVAILABLE IN SOFTCOVER OR HARDCOVER WITH DUST JACKET

ESCAPE FROM THE FRENCH *by Edward Boys*—A Young Royal Navy Midshipman's Adventures During the Napoleonic War.

THE VOYAGE OF H.M.S. PANDORA *by Edward Edwards R. N. & George Hamilton, edited by Basil Thomson*—In Pursuit of the Mutineers of the Bounty in the South Seas—1790-1791.

MEDUSA *by J. B. Henry Savigny and Alexander Correard and Charlotte-Adélaïde Dard* —Narrative of a Voyage to Senegal in 1816 & The Sufferings of the Picard Family After the Shipwreck of the Medusa.

THE SEA WAR OF 1812 VOLUME 1 *by A. T. Mahan*—A History of the Maritime Conflict.

THE SEA WAR OF 1812 VOLUME 2 *by A. T. Mahan*—A History of the Maritime Conflict.

WETHERELL OF H. M. S. HUSSAR *by John Wetherell*—The Recollections of an Ordinary Seaman of the Royal Navy During the Napoleonic Wars.

THE NAVAL BRIGADE IN NATAL *by C. R. N. Burne*—With the Guns of H. M. S. Terrible & H. M. S. Tartar during the Boer War 1899-1900.

THE VOYAGE OF H. M. S. BOUNTY *by William Bligh*—The True Story of an 18th Century Voyage of Exploration and Mutiny.

SHIPWRECK! *by William Gilly*—The Royal Navy's Disasters at Sea 1793-1849.

KING'S CUTTERS AND SMUGGLERS: 1700-1855 *by E. Keble Chatterton*—A unique period of maritime history-from the beginning of the eighteenth to the middle of the nineteenth century when British seamen risked all to smuggle valuable goods from wool to tea and spirits from and to the Continent.

CONFEDERATE BLOCKADE RUNNER *by John Wilkinson*—The Personal Recollections of an Officer of the Confederate Navy.

NAVAL BATTLES OF THE NAPOLEONIC WARS *by W. H. Fitchett*—Cape St. Vincent, the Nile, Cadiz, Copenhagen, Trafalgar & Others.

PRISONERS OF THE RED DESERT *by R. S. Gwatkin-Williams*—The Adventures of the Crew of the Tara During the First World War.

U-BOAT WAR 1914-1918 *by James B. Connolly/Karl von Schenk*—Two Contrasting Accounts from Both Sides of the Conflict at Sea D uring the Great War.

AVAILABLE ONLINE AT www.leonaur.com
AND FROM ALL GOOD BOOK STORES

07/09

LEONAUR

ALSO FROM LEONAUR
AVAILABLE IN SOFTCOVER OR HARDCOVER WITH DUST JACKET

IRON TIMES WITH THE GUARDS *by An O. E. (G. P. A. Fildes)*—The Experiences of an Officer of the Coldstream Guards on the Western Front During the First World War.

THE GREAT WAR IN THE MIDDLE EAST: 1 *by W. T. Massey*—The Desert Campaigns & How Jerusalem Was Won---two classic accounts in one volume.

THE GREAT WAR IN THE MIDDLE EAST: 2 *by W. T. Massey*—Allenby's Final Triumph.

SMITH-DORRIEN *by Horace Smith-Dorrien*—Isandlwhana to the Great War.

1914 *by Sir John French*—The Early Campaigns of the Great War by the British Commander.

GRENADIER *by E. R. M. Fryer*—The Recollections of an Officer of the Grenadier Guards throughout the Great War on the Western Front.

BATTLE, CAPTURE & ESCAPE *by George Pearson*—The Experiences of a Canadian Light Infantryman During the Great War.

DIGGERS AT WAR *by R. Hugh Knyvett & G. P. Cuttriss*—"Over There" With the Australians by R. Hugh Knyvett and Over the Top With the Third Australian Division by G. P. Cuttriss. Accounts of Australians During the Great War in the Middle East, at Gallipoli and on the Western Front.

HEAVY FIGHTING BEFORE US *by George Brenton Laurie*—The Letters of an Officer of the Royal Irish Rifles on the Western Front During the Great War.

THE CAMELIERS *by Oliver Hogue*—A Classic Account of the Australians of the Imperial Camel Corps During the First World War in the Middle East.

RED DUST *by Donald Black*—A Classic Account of Australian Light Horsemen in Palestine During the First World War.

THE LEAN, BROWN MEN *by Angus Buchanan*—Experiences in East Africa During the Great War with the 25th Royal Fusiliers—the Legion of Frontiersmen.

THE NIGERIAN REGIMENT IN EAST AFRICA *by W. D. Downes*—On Campaign During the Great War 1916-1918.

THE 'DIE-HARDS' IN SIBERIA *by John Ward*—With the Middlesex Regiment Against the Bolsheviks 1918-19.

AVAILABLE ONLINE AT www.leonaur.com
AND FROM ALL GOOD BOOK STORES

07/09

LEONAUR

ALSO FROM LEONAUR

AVAILABLE IN SOFTCOVER OR HARDCOVER WITH DUST JACKET

FARAWAY CAMPAIGN *by F. James*—Experiences of an Indian Army Cavalry Officer in Persia & Russia During the Great War.

REVOLT IN THE DESERT *by T. E. Lawrence*—An account of the experiences of one remarkable British officer's war from his own perspective.

MACHINE-GUN SQUADRON *by A. M. G.*—The 20th Machine Gunners from British Yeomanry Regiments in the Middle East Campaign of the First World War.

A GUNNER'S CRUSADE *by Antony Bluett*—The Campaign in the Desert, Palestine & Syria as Experienced by the Honourable Artillery Company During the Great War .

DESPATCH RIDER *by W. H. L. Watson*—The Experiences of a British Army Motorcycle Despatch Rider During the Opening Battles of the Great War in Europe.

TIGERS ALONG THE TIGRIS *by E. J. Thompson*—The Leicestershire Regiment in Mesopotamia During the First World War.

HEARTS & DRAGONS *by Charles R. M. F. Crutwell*—The 4th Royal Berkshire Regiment in France and Italy During the Great War, 1914-1918.

INFANTRY BRIGADE: 1914 *by John Ward*—The Diary of a Commander of the 15th Infantry Brigade, 5th Division, British Army, During the Retreat from Mons.

DOING OUR 'BIT' *by Ian Hay*—Two Classic Accounts of the Men of Kitchener's 'New Army' During the Great War including *The First 100,000 & All In It.*

AN EYE IN THE STORM *by Arthur Ruhl*—An American War Correspondent's Experiences of the First World War from the Western Front to Gallipoli-and Beyond.

STAND & FALL *by Joe Cassells*—With the Middlesex Regiment Against the Bolsheviks 1918-19.

RIFLEMAN MACGILL'S WAR *by Patrick MacGill*—A Soldier of the London Irish During the Great War in Europe including *The Amateur Army, The Red Horizon & The Great Push.*

WITH THE GUNS *by C. A. Rose & Hugh Dalton*—Two First Hand Accounts of British Gunners at War in Europe During World War 1- Three Years in France with the Guns and With the British Guns in Italy.

THE BUSH WAR DOCTOR *by Robert V. Dolbey*—The Experiences of a British Army Doctor During the East African Campaign of the First World War.

AVAILABLE ONLINE AT **www.leonaur.com**
AND FROM ALL GOOD BOOK STORES

07/09

LEONAUR

ALSO FROM LEONAUR
AVAILABLE IN SOFTCOVER OR HARDCOVER WITH DUST JACKET

THE 9TH—THE KING'S (LIVERPOOL REGIMENT) IN THE GREAT WAR 1914 - 1918 *by Enos H. G. Roberts*—Mersey to mud—war and Liverpool men.

THE GAMBARDIER *by Mark Severn*—The experiences of a battery of Heavy artillery on the Western Front during the First World War.

FROM MESSINES TO THIRD YPRES *by Thomas Floyd*—A personal account of the First World War on the Western front by a 2/5th Lancashire Fusilier.

THE IRISH GUARDS IN THE GREAT WAR - VOLUME 1 *by Rudyard Kipling*—Edited and Compiled from Their Diaries and Papers—The First Battalion.

THE IRISH GUARDS IN THE GREAT WAR - VOLUME 1 *by Rudyard Kipling*—Edited and Compiled from Their Diaries and Papers—The Second Battalion.

ARMOURED CARS IN EDEN *by K. Roosevelt*—An American President's son serving in Rolls Royce armoured cars with the British in Mesopatamia & with the American Artillery in France during the First World War.

CHASSEUR OF 1914 *by Marcel Dupont*—Experiences of the twilight of the French Light Cavalry by a young officer during the early battles of the great war in Europe.

TROOP HORSE & TRENCH *by R.A. Lloyd*—The experiences of a British Lifeguardsman of the household cavalry fighting on the western front during the First World War 1914-18.

THE EAST AFRICAN MOUNTED RIFLES *by C.J. Wilson*—Experiences of the campaign in the East African bush during the First World War.

THE LONG PATROL *by George Berrie*—A Novel of Light Horsemen from Gallipoli to the Palestine campaign of the First World War.

THE FIGHTING CAMELIERS *by Frank Reid*—The exploits of the Imperial Camel Corps in the desert and Palestine campaigns of the First World War.

STEEL CHARIOTS IN THE DESERT *by S. C. Rolls*—The first world war experiences of a Rolls Royce armoured car driver with the Duke of Westminster in Libya and in Arabia with T.E. Lawrence.

WITH THE IMPERIAL CAMEL CORPS IN THE GREAT WAR *by Geoffrey Inchbald*—The story of a serving officer with the British 2nd battalion against the Senussi and during the Palestine campaign.

AVAILABLE ONLINE AT **www.leonaur.com**
AND FROM ALL GOOD BOOK STORES

07/09

CPSIA information can be obtained at www.ICGtesting.com
Printed in the USA
LVOW060303080413

328054LV00001B/54/P